MW00333029

The
Heart
of
Teaching

Advanced praise for The Heart of Teaching

"Lisa Lee genuinely writes from the heart. Her stories—the ones that evoke laughter and the ones that may elicit a few tears—capture both the spirit and the complexities of what it means and how it feels to be a teacher. Lee's narrative not only allows readers an opportunity to refl ect on their own experi ences, but encourages them (this reader, at least) to be better teachers and better people."

-Jen Webb

"In this book, Lisa Lee gives us permission to fall in love with (or fall back in love with) teaching. In a climate where educators feel uncertain of the response they will receive when stating their profession, Lisa Lee audaciously declares, "I've loved teaching for over 30 years, and guess what? I STILL love it"! Inspiration, enthusiasm, passion, humor – if these are words you think no longer apply to the educational environment, read this book."

- S. Dugger

"Lisa Lee's passion for educating and connecting with her students shines through in her stories, which are told with humor and grace. I'm so grateful for all of the teachers like Lisa, who are making a diff erence in the lives of so many kids, our future."

- Ali Lasell

Advanced praise for The Heart of Teaching

"Lisa Lee truly delves into what it means to get to the heart of teaching. Between her extensive experience being an attentive, loving educator and advocate in her students' lives, to her incredibly eclectic collection of life experiences, she takes her audience along for a journey through the ages of teaching. The shifts and changes she shows in the educational landscape that she artfully moved between throughout her stories show just how incredible of a teacher, storyteller, and person she is.

Lisa Lee has created an artfully masterful narrative in The Heart of Teaching. Her stories, while humorous, touching, and emotional, will also take you through an exploration of the development of education through multiple decades. Between her experience as an educator, as well as an incredibly supportive person throughout her life, her stories will bring you back to a simpler time in education, and have you learning like so many others have in their time with her through the years."

-Elliott Holm

"Lisa approaches this book in the same way she approaches her teaching. She uses humor, respect, caring and her own life experiences to guide the readers through the pages. Her stories provide the reader a very extensive telling of life as a new teacher. You see, hear, and live the experiences of her journey to becoming a master teacher. Her story is the story of so many nameless, dedicated, and loving teachers in this country. Lisa has put into words the many faces of teaching in a public school."

- Bill Duncan

The Heart of Teaching

LISA LEE

Mind Flash Publishing
an Imprint of Journey Institute Press

Mind Flash Publishing
An imprint of Journey Institute Press,
a division of 50 in 52 Journey, Inc.
journeyinstitute.org/press

Library of Congress Control Number: 2022946551
Name: Lee, Lisa
Title: The Heart of Teaching
Description: Colorado: Mind Flash Publishing, 2022
Identifiers: ISBN 978-1-7373591-6-6 (hardcover)
Subjects: BISAC: EDUCATION / Teaching / Methods & Strategies |
EDUCATION / Philosophy, Theory & Social Aspects |
EDUCATION / Inclusive Education.

First Edition

Printed in the United States of America

This book was typeset in Baskerville URW, Casnu

To the one I love a "whole much," Cyndy Hampton. You're my greatest source of strength, and you've made this dream a reality. You are forever my person, and I sure am glad we chose to go left at the fork. No book will ever be as special as our story.

And

To Margot/Margarine, James Patrick, and Bev-o, my family of choice. Thank you for believing in me long before I believed in myself. I love you so.

Contents

Foreword

I often find that a book's Introduction is the best indicator of whether the author whose work I'm about to read is going to capture and sustain my attention. It's in the Introduction that the author's intent for writing their book becomes apparent (or doesn't), and it's in the Introduction that you first notice if an author's voice is genuine, and their knowledge of and respect for their topic sincere. In the case of Lisa Lee's The Heart of Teaching I defy you to not want to dig into every page of her book, as this "real teacher" (as Lisa calls herself) lays before you a treasure trove of insights into a profession that she loves.

Lisa hopes that as you read her book you feel that you are actually sitting beside her having a conversation. That is exactly how I felt! Having the privilege of knowing Lisa for many years, as well as having had the honor of teaching her high school students during a visit to her classroom at Wheat Ridge High School in Colorado, I've come to see first-hand not only how she affects her students in countless ways, but how they affect her as well. Each of her book's essays is awash with tales of wonder, strife and every possible human emotion that occurs in a classroom when there is the type of magic that Lisa Lee creates through her teaching... through her being.

Lisa recollects her early days of teaching, when mimeograph machines left the user purple-fingered, connecting them to the present, when today's technology is advanced. in ways that educators of yesteryear couldn't even imagine. Even with these changes, though, Lisa reminds us that there remains one constant: our students look to their teachers for hope, reassurance, gentle (and sometimes, rigorous) prodding to try something challenging, and a vision of what is possible in their lives. Lisa Lee's humorous, tear-jerking and brutally honest recollections of her 30+ years as a teacher show her to be the type of educator every parent wants their children to experience, even once, in their K-12 career.

Later in her Introduction, Lisa compares teachers to Superheroes, stating that the reason people so admire them is that they inspire hope that mere mortals might not be so able to do. The best of teachers--teachers like Lisa Lee--actually are Superheroes in the eyes of the kindergartener just beginning to read or the 12th grader seeking reassurance that there is life beyond high school. You'll come to realize just how much of a Superhero Lisa Lee is as you experience the wisdom and beauty of The Heart of Teaching. So, pony up a glass or cup of your favorite beverage: you're about to have a wonderful conversation with one of education's best, Lisa Lee.

Jim Delisle, Ph.D.
Professor, Author, Teacher

Introduction

Dear Reader,

Thank you for choosing to pick up my book. Whether you realize it or not, you're holding my heart in your hands. For as long as I can remember, there was never anything I wanted to do more than work with kids. It was something that came from within—it grew with me—and it has always seemed to be as much a part of my DNA as my hair color. Over a career that has spanned almost four decades, there has never been a time when I doubted my choice. Teaching was just what I had to do. I've watched the profession evolve and change in so many ways. I still have strong arm muscles from cranking old mimeograph machines, while now I just push a button and my copies emerge. When I first began teaching, "Take out your notebook" had a much different meaning than it does today! Handwriting lessons have been replaced with keyboarding classes. Yet the one constant through all the years and all the changes has been the sense of wholeness I feel when in the classroom. I am at my best there.

As I wrote, one question kept coming up, both from myself and from those who were reading over my initial drafts. *Who is the intended audience?* My response changed from one day of writing to the next, and I finally decided that there was no one answer to the question. Sometimes, I wrote to those considering a career in education, hoping it would inspire them to take the leap. On other days, my intended audience was veteran educators who needed a reminder of the incredibly important work we do. During some writing sessions, I just wrote for all of those whose lives have been impacted by educators. And then there were times when I just wrote for the pure enjoyment of reliving these memories, hoping they would entertain my readers at least a little. All I knew was that these stories needed to be told, these children needed to be known, and the lessons I learned needed to be passed on.

As you read my words, I hope you'll feel like I'm sitting beside you having a conversation. I hope you'll laugh with me, cry with me, and celebrate this profession that affects all of us in one way or another. Over the last few decades, I've watched the pressures from outside the profession increase. Although public education has always been government funded, it has been politicized today in ways I never imagined through unfunded mandates, educator evaluations, budget cuts, and curriculum controversies. As I've watched many colleagues permanently turn off their classroom lights far earlier than they'd planned as the outside influences became too much to bear, I can't help but think of the many students they could have touched and been touched by. In a time when educators are vilified, when every person running for elected office is an "expert" on what education should look like, teaching is not for the faint of heart, not that it ever was. Education colleges across the nation are enrolling fewer and fewer students, and some programs have been permanently eliminated. More and more teachers are leaving the profession, and this cornerstone of American society is in crisis. Yet the need for good teachers is as strong as it ever was. Sometimes, it feels like nothing short of a miracle that I've maintained my energy, love for teaching, and sense of humor over the years. But I guess the miracle has come in the form of the students who have come my way. You will be hearing from some of them in the form of quotes and "I Am" poems. It didn't make sense to write this book without letting them have a voice. After all, it's their story as much as it is mine.

I began teaching in 1987, and in my nearly forty-year career, I can't think of a demographic or age I haven't taught. I began in a school surrounded by pastureland, followed by one deep in the inner city. I've walked the halls with students who came from homes of privilege, as well as those who told tales of growing up in refugee camps. I've attended the ballet recitals of my kindergartners and the proms of my high schoolers. I've taught at schools where over forty languages were spoken and those with no need for second-language programs. No matter the circumstances, I've loved and taught them to the best of my ability.

Every year since August 1987, I get butterflies when I walk into a store and see shiny, just-waiting-to-be-opened school supplies prominently displayed. I've always said that I'd know it was time to retire when the butterflies didn't come. I'm still waiting. For me, the pencils, composition books, and glue speak of the promise of unexplored opportunities, new relationships to forge, and endless memories waiting to be made. As I pass by the hand sanitizer, calculators, and tissue boxes, I think about the laughter that will soon be filling my classroom, of the tears I'll shed while reading a personal narrative. I reflect on the exhilaration that is ahead, which consistently outweighs the exhaustion.

After teaching hundreds and hundreds of students, after hour upon hour of lesson planning and grading, after more parent-teacher conferences than I could ever count, I come to you with one message: it has all been worth it. And I wish I could guarantee every educator a career such as the one I have experienced. As you turn the pages, I hope that what comes through more than anything else is that teaching is a calling, one that takes us on a journey that—while full of plenty of bumps in the road—ultimately changes our lives and shapes who we are.

All these years later, I have no regrets. When I look back, I have memories ranging from teaching pre-K to elementary to middle to high school. I think about the learning centers, the student performances, the educational conferences, the field trips, the report card deadlines, and the evaluations. I think about all of the hours spent supervising students at lunch duty, recess duty, bus duty, and hall duty. I'll never forget the nights spent grading into the wee hours of the morning, and the endless hours of professional development. I'm overwhelmed by all the memories. Come, walk with me through the years. Experience the tears, the laughter, and the pure enjoyment that only this profession can bring.

But before you begin, I have to be completely honest. I almost didn't write this book—but not because I didn't think I had a story to tell or because I felt my message about the importance of teachers wasn't vital. I worried that by telling the story of my teaching journey, I'd come across as though I think I'm the "One With All The Answers," which is far from the truth. These pages are filled with fun, laughter, and joy, but I could have written just as much about the lessons I've learned from my mistakes. In putting this all into words, I've fretted that others won't be able to relate to this extroverted, eccentric, chaotically energetic educator. Superheroes are fictional, benevolent characters with superhuman powers, something that is unattainable for us mere humans, but I think one of the main reasons superheroes are so popular is because they symbolize hope in an unpredictable world. Our students so often come to us in need of such hope, craving a connection with someone who sees and values them for who they are. Those of us in this profession certainly need positivity and hope, maybe now more than ever before. From critical race theory to sex education and gender identity issues—curriculum disputes plague our profession. On top of the ever-present threats to funding and job security, we now must deal with the way Covid has forever changed the educational landscape. The expectations and demands seem to grow every year, with little to balance out the stress.

For the last several decades, I've had a tagline on my work email: "I didn't choose the wrong profession. Society chose the wrong heroes." This may seem contradictory given what I just wrote about superheroes. The truth is, I *do* see teachers as heroes. Our villains come in the form of initiatives, such as those that force us to post lesson plans a year ahead of time. While we don't have to leap tall buildings in a single bound, we *do* have to jump through the hoops of whatever shiny new initiative is thrust upon us any given year. Capes are not typically part of our daily attire, but multiple hats certainly are: teacher, counselor, nurse, therapist, custodian, guard, comedian, actor, mediator, lawyer, judge, sage, artist, coach, doctor, parent, event planner, motivator, life coach, drill sergeant, detective, social worker, negotiator, referee, cheerleader, entreprenuer, decorator. Can you think of any other profession that requires so much from those in the trenches? What we do is truly heroic. (But on a personal note, I'm grateful that we don't have to wear tights and bodysuits!)

And what do all superheroes ultimately hope to accomplish? They work to keep others safe, they rescue those in danger, and they save lives. They strive to make the world a better place. I think that pretty much sums up what teachers do day after day, don't you? There is no one right way to be a life-changing educator. My way won't be your way, nor should it be. Our teaching styles are as unique and individual as our fingerprints. I just hope my story will leave you with the certainty that teachers can and *do* change lives.

With love and gratitude,

Lisa Lee, Real Teacher

Chapter 1

Real Teachers: Touch the Heart, Teach the Mind

"On Teaching"

It is customary for adults to forget how hard and dull school is. The learning by memory all the basic things one must know is the most incredible and unending effort. Learning to read is probably the most difficult and revolutionary thing that happens to the human brain and if you don't believe that, watch an illiterate adult try to do it. School is not so easy, and it is not for the most part very fun, but then, if you are very lucky you may find a teacher. Three real teachers in a lifetime is the very best of luck. I have come to believe that a great teacher is a great artist and that there are as few as there are any other great artists. Teaching might even be the greatest of the arts since the medium is the human mind and spirit. My three had this in common. They all loved what they were doing. They did not tell—they catalyzed a burning desire to know. Under their influence, the horizons sprung wide and fear went away and the unknown became knowable. But most important of all, the truth, that dangerous stuff, became beautiful and precious.

—John Steinbeck

Years ago, when I read Steinbeck's thoughts about "real teachers" for the first time, I cried. They still move me, regardless of how many times I've read, written, or spoken them. I only recently learned the story behind his words, however. In his essay "Like Captured Fireflies," Steinbeck writes that his eleven-year-old son came to him and morosely asked how much longer he had to stay in school. Steinbeck was met with horror when he predicted his son likely had fifteen or more years of schooling ahead. He then told his child about the "real teachers" he himself had encountered as a student, describing them as "great artists."

Over time, I have decided that great artists and teachers have a lot in common. They have a sense of adventure and a willingness to try new things. They know how to be flexible and not take themselves too seriously. Real artists and teachers have a desire to grow in the areas that hold them back from further developing their craft. But above all else, they are dedicated and passionate about their work. They have no choice but to create—it is who they are at their very core. Making art is a necessity for them.

I've spent almost four decades in the studio of the mind. In no way have I been a perfect teacher, but I have tried to be the best I could be at any given moment. I have tried to transform each student's canvas into the most exquisite work of fine art possible, to be admired and appreciated for the ages. And although Steinbeck writes about the teacher as an artist, the truth is that educators are also transformed by those they teach. Over the years, my talent as an artist of the mind and spirit has been honed through the students who have passed through my classroom. The primary students who looked to me for far more than a reading or math lesson guided my brushstrokes, and they added color and depth that I didn't know were missing in my life. As I worked to sculpt my hormones-with-legs middle school students, they chiseled me into something different and better than I was before they entered my life. In my high school classroom, we were all shaped and molded on the potter's wheel of never-ending teenage energy and idealism.

The palettes continually changed. Some years were a bit abstract, while others were more realistic than I might have liked. But when they're all put together, the experiences create a gallery that fills me with gratitude and pride.

When I started college, I was ready to fulfill my life's dream of working with kids, and I envisioned myself working in or running my own children's home. I even spent time in an orphanage in Haiti for a bit. I started off with a social work major, but I decided there wasn't enough focus on children, so I changed to child and family development. I didn't even consider majoring in education—I'm not sure why, but I was so focused on having my own children's home that it never crossed my mind. But only six months after receiving my undergraduate degree, I found myself working on my master's degree in early childhood education. I had NO desire to teach anyone who came above my elbow, and for fifteen years, it never happened. Well, some of my fourth graders came almost to my shoulder, but I never even considered venturing into the world of tweens, even though I was certified to teach up to sixth grade. When we'd pass the older grades in the halls, I'd keep my littles as far away from them as possible in case any of their "bigness" contaminated us.

After fifteen fulfilling years of hanging out with short people, I began teaching in the gifted and talented field. It was a bit intimidating because I'd be working with students in second through sixth grade—I'd be teaching in enemy territory when those fifth and sixth graders darkened my door! I just figured that I'd enjoy my time with the second, third, and fourth graders enough that the time I had to spend with the Big Kids would be less painful. Boy, was I surprised! Those ten-, eleven-, and twelve-year-olds Changed. My. Life. I LOVED them! I found myself eagerly awaiting the days that those tall kids walked into my suite of classrooms.

Yes, I said suite . . . I had two small adjoining classrooms, and my fifth graders came up with the idea of painting the walls of both rooms with colorful murals. They chose an African village theme and painted one room with safari, jungle, and wild animal daylight scenes. That became the room in which we did our more traditional work. We created nocturnal scenes in the other room and built a hut that we filled with lamps, pillows, and couches. That became the hangout space where we read together, debated, and solved the problems of the world. They invited the younger students to participate in the painting, and the work we all put into the transformation resulted in such a sense of belonging. We truly grew into a village in which everyone had a voice, and we spent our days acting out Greek myths, exploring our genealogy, and learning about mindfulness before that was even a buzzword. We took part in a Relay for Life event where we spent an entire night walking a high school track over and over to raise money for cancer research. Students became characters in a wax museum, which the rest of the school toured to learn about influential Americans. By the end of the year, it was hard to imagine how I'd ever managed to teach without those older kids.

Yet even this idyllic world was hit with the reality that comes with the dreaded FTE, or full-time equivalent, a calculation showing how many students would be attending an individual school if they were all enrolled full time. My position at that school was going to be reduced to part time the next year, and I'd need to find another part-time position if I wanted to continue working with the community I'd grown to love. I'd never had to consider splitting my time between more than one school, and it was a bit daunting. I had always thrown myself wholeheartedly into the community where I was teaching. The families became friends; the faculty became family. As I was exploring options, my principal told me about a full-time GT position teaching seventh- and eighth-grade social studies at the highest-profile middle school in the district. Naturally, I said, "Not today, Satan!" Not only would it involve teaching even taller students, but I also wasn't certified to teach above grade six. Not to mention that this was one of the highest-performing schools in the state—one that was often in the public eye. Just the thought of it made me want to apply at the local Home Depot. My principal just shook his head, smiled, and said, "But Lisa, you'd be so *good* at it." I reluctantly threw my hat into the ring, convinced I'd be passed over for consideration since I didn't have the proper credentials. Was I ever gobsmacked when human resources called to set up a time for me to interview with the principal the following week. In fact, when I answered the phone, I asked them if they had called the right number!

Right before the interview, as luck would have it, I broke my foot. So, on a stormy April afternoon, I found myself hobbling on my crutches through the doors of a *middle school* to talk about a job I had no interest in taking, my lack of qualifications notwithstanding. I wasn't the only one with doubts. The principal greeted me, and we headed back to her office. As soon as I got myself and my crutches situated, she said that she was confused as to why HR had sent me over because I wasn't qualified for the position. Before she could finish, I found myself nodding my head emphatically in agreement, and then I blurted out, "I don't even *like* middle school students! I think you should pepper spray them every morning and be done with it, because they're gonna earn it before the day is out." To this day, I'm still not sure whether or not she thought I was serious (I was), but the principal burst into uncontrollable laughter. When she could manage a breath, she sputtered out something about me not knowing that I was a born middle school teacher. By the end of the interview (most of which consisted of her trying to convince me to take the position and me telling her all the reasons not to hire me), she'd committed to paying for any certifications I needed to be able to work for her the next fall.

That's just what happened, and to my absolute shock, I've never looked back. (And did you know that middle school teachers go straight to heaven? That was a bonus I wasn't aware of, but it became an incentive to stay when you had a day that more closely resembled the *other place*.) In fact, after just a year, I found myself in certification classes so I'd be able to follow my students into high school if I wanted to—I couldn't get enough of those angsty, hilarious, hormonal kids! They were just so *real*. I have trouble explaining just what that means. Imagine squeezing a wad of terracotta clay in your hand. Let it ooze through your fingers. (Insert squelching, wet sounds here.) The clay represents the kids . . . they are just so . . . *there*, in all their smelly, clumsy, malleable glory. Even now, when I've had priceless years of experience teaching high school, not to mention the many glorious ones with elementary students . . . those middle school humans are still my favorite people to teach. Even though they are taller than the students I once preferred.

I Am

I am crazy and strong.
I wonder about who I really am
I hear giant dinosaur footsteps
I see a black shadow stalking me
I am crazy and strong
I want whatever I wish to come true
I am crazy and strong.
I pretend to be invincible
I feel like someone is in distress
I touch the hands of the lost
I worry that we will move
I cry when my dog eats Mr. Sandwich
I am crazy and strong.
I understand that I am smart
I say Godzilla is real
I dream that I'm eating Jimmy John's and going to Target
I try hard at math
I hope I get a Skull Crawler toy
I am crazy and strong.

—Sebastian, age nine

Chapter 2

Riding the Waves

Tybee Island, off the coast of Savannah, Georgia, is one of the happiest places on earth for me. But if you're looking for pristine, clear water, don't even waste your time. You should head further south to Florida and check out Siesta Key instead. You won't find the beautiful shades of azure waters on Tybee. Instead, the island is surrounded by such grayish-brown water that it's sometimes difficult to see your feet even when you're wading in the shallows. One reason for the murkiness is the earth's rotation, which can cause sediment to shift, thereby muddying things up. However, these waters are also rich in nutrients, thanks to the living organisms riding the waves, skidding along the ocean floor, and churning onto the shore. Along with their food sources, the organisms inhabiting these waters make the ocean cloudy. Anyone who's felt the sting of a jellyfish, trod upon a hermit crab shell, or felt something brush against their legs while jumping the waves, has experienced an ocean that's teeming with life. Although the beauty of a teal blue ocean stretching out to the horizon can take my breath away, give me the grey waters any day . . . They're ALIVE.

When I was still new to teaching, trying to navigate the world of first grade in an inner-city neighborhood, there was a third-grade teacher in my building whose classroom management skills were revered by the administration as the gold standard for the rest of us. The fact that you could hear a pin drop in her classroom was considered highly commendable. When she walked her students down the hall, their soft footfalls were hardly discernible. She likely never suffered from "teacher kidneys" because she could—the biggest miracle of all—leave her class alone while she went to the *adult* bathroom!

I, meanwhile, felt I'd had a successful day if no one had used Elmer's glue along with hair they had surreptitiously cut from their classmate's heads to give themselves a mustache! (Trust me, safety scissors are sharper than you know.) If we made it back from a bathroom break without leaving a monochromatic mural behind on the wall (use your imagination, or better yet, don't; again, just trust me), it was a cause for celebration. I began to strongly consider keeping a box of Depends right next to the Kleenex because leaving those six-year-olds alone for a bathroom break was as unthinkable as asking my grandmama why her teeth were kept in a jar . . . it just wasn't a good idea. And while this teacher had substitutes lining up to work for her, I was never able to get the same one to come back twice. MY subs left *pages* that detailed their experience, with words like "wild," "uncivilized," and "NeverEverAgain" scattered throughout the paragraphs. I knew that having the classroom control that She Who Could Do No Wrong had wasn't ever going to be in the cards for me. Other, tamer occupations began to look appealing. Need someone to taste test which laxatives are more palatable? I'm your girl! Training to become a body piercer? I have lots of space to work with.

Mine was the classroom that interrupted other classes throughout the building. When we walked the halls on the way to lunch or PE, doors slammed shut in our wake. Forget hearing a pin drop in our space; I'm not sure the grenade attached to the pin would have registered on most days. The orderly classroom management gene had passed me by; I was never even in its orbit. Yet I came back, day after day, no matter the mayhem and pandemonium. And the truth began to slowly dawn on me. I realized I actually looked forward to the cheerful chaos that would ensue the moment the school doors opened every morning. I began to see enormous progress happening; my students were voluntarily consuming entire books. I noticed that they were constantly smiling. Their ebullient laughter was surpassed only by their thirst for learning. Somehow, in spite of everything, we figured out a way to make *us* work. I never received high marks on my evaluations for classroom management or organization. But you know what you *would* find in our classroom, something that no evaluation instrument could capture? The joy of learning. Oh, my, there was so much life in those four walls.

Over thirty-five years of tides ebbing and flowing have come and gone since those days, a blur of sunshine and hurricanes. I've taught students who were born in refugee camps, and I've worked with those who came from homes of great privilege. I've ridden the waves with elementary, middle, and high schoolers. I've grown and evolved as an educator, shaped by my students as surely as a rocky cliff is shaped by the ocean. As the decades have passed, my hair has grayed, wrinkles have formed, and I bear little physical resemblance to that young teacher. But the treasure she discovered washed up in the hallways of an inner-city Atlanta school has never diminished over time. Teaching is chaotic. It is messy. But I've never sought out the calm, pristine, clear waters . . . I prefer the grit, the unknown lurking beneath the surface, the unpredictability of what the next day will bring. Because, as we get tossed and turned by the waves, we are consumed with the knowledge that we are surrounded by LIFE.

I Am

I am cool and kind
I wonder why Ameila Earhart vanished
I hear a T-Rex roaring
I see Godzilla doing the Floss
I want my own cruise ship
I am cool and kind.
I pretend to be John Cena
I feel a thousand nails poking me in my side
I touched a dinosaur tooth and it came out
I worry about another Ice Age and tornadoes
I cry when I think about my mom dying
I am cool and kind.
I understand I will never have a billion dollars
I say people who kill rhinos, crocodiles, and pythons for their
skins should STOP
I dream about being the best football player
I try hard to get completions at football
I hope there's no more protesting about laws
I am cool and kind.

-Jack, age 8

Chapter 3

The Times, They Are A-changin'!

When I began teaching, students would tell me I was like a second mom to them. As I aged, I became like a favorite aunt. Eventually, I evolved into being like their grandma. I was quite frightened about what moniker might be next, so I finally became "Mama Lee" to everyone. That worked for me and kept me feeling young. But my titles aren't the only things that have changed.

When I first started teaching, if I wanted to make copies, my arm was guaranteed a workout as I cranked the handle on the mimeograph machine, watching as it spat out wet purple worksheets. My students loved to get them hot off the press, holding the warm papers to their noses and inhaling the lingering chemical scent. When the mimeograph machine gave way to fancy copiers, we were so excited, only to find that they seemed to be forever jammed or out of toner. And if you wanted to cause a major breakdown, you'd be sure to choose the staple option.

Classroom technology involved an overhead projector, markers, and film. When document cameras hit the market, I felt like the very definition of the modern teacher! We had filmstrip projectors that we carefully threaded with 35 mm spooled film. I can still remember the feel of the film as I unrolled it from its red plastic canister. After only a few years, the filmstrip projectors were overtaken by videocassettes. Teachers shared rolling TV and VHS carts, and heaven forbid if we needed one at the same time as another teacher! The TVs were secured to the top of the carts with heavy black nylon bands, but every year, we'd be warned about their tendency to be top heavy, and gruesome stories about them toppling over onto children kept all of us on our toes.

Computers didn't enter the picture until I had been teaching for over a decade. When report card time rolled around, I faced weekends filled with hand-calculating grades for every single student in every single class. When I discovered those "E-Z Graders, which easily translated the number of wrong answers into an overall grade, I was in awe. I finally joined modern society and bought a calculator for averaging grades, but even using that to average grades still took more time than I can begin to say. I lived in fear of losing my gradebook—an actual, spiral-bound notebook with neatly lined green pages that contained columns for each day of the week and lines for each child in the class—the one and only record of grades for a quarter's or semester's worth of work. When I heard that there were computer systems being developed that would average grades digitally, I swear it felt like I'd just followed Dr. Who through the Tardis!

Technology also brought changes to lesson planning and research. Need to find a book from the library that relates to a unit you want to teach? Got a student who has a topic to research? The handy dandy card catalog, complete with the Dewey decimal system, was your friend, even though none of us understood how it worked. If I was looking for specific information, I'd check out six or seven books in hopes that between all of them, I might be able to piece together a lesson plan. It was such a pain to lug a heavy satchel of books back and forth from school to home with me every night, yet when I search the library's database for books today, it's just not the same. Uploading articles into my Google drive or printing out news articles that I located with a ten-second search doesn't compare to the feel of thumbing through those drawers of little white cards, reveling in the adventures, beautiful places, and magical creatures contained within those narrow spaces.

In the 1980s and early '90s, only the Very Important People like the principals, secretaries, and custodians had walkie-talkies. When a teacher got a call at school, they'd be summoned over the intercom: "Mrs. So and So, you have a phone call in the office." A mad scramble would ensue as we tried to get someone to cover the class, followed by a hurried jog to the office, all while hoping that whoever it was on the phone hadn't hung up in the twenty minutes it took to get there. If we had a classroom emergency, there were no phones with twirly cords to dial the office. If something happened to one of our students, we just chose the kid with the fastest legs to hightail it to the office for help while we did our best to get the blood flow under control or stood guard over the misbehaving student. And while we're on the subject of emergencies, there was no such thing as a school nurse. Our secretaries were the first line of defense, and we counted on them to dole out medication, bag up ice for sprains, and stop bloody noses in between pounding out staff memos on their fancy electric typewriters and answering the phone—the kind with the twirly cords.

Something I wasn't prepared for prior to becoming a teacher was how often I'd need to call upon my non-existent artistic ability. It seemed that every wall was covered by that blasted brown corkboard, just waiting to terrorize—I mean inspire—me to greatness. If you were "lucky" enough to have a bulletin board in the hallway outside of your classroom, you were expected to keep it decorated. And updated. I would literally lie awake at night thinking about what my next bulletin board should be. Sometimes I tried to make myself dream about what my next creation would look like, and it actually worked once or twice. True story. As much as I enjoyed the changing of the seasons, I dreaded the ever-present need to design a colorful, neat seasonal display. For a (mercifully) few years, interactive bulletin boards became the rage. All of our displays had to have some type of lesson or game with which students could interact.

While my creative energy rarely let me down, I never received any awards for my artistic ability. I have a vivid memory of being observed by the professor in charge of my student teaching practicum while teaching a math lesson to a class of first graders. I had laboriously cut out pictures of fruit from construction paper over several hours and was so proud of the results. Until, that is, I proudly flourished a stack of yellow bananas to start the lesson, and my student Elizabeth just said, "Whoa." Total silence. My professor was the first to crack, and then the rest of us were holding our sides, laughing at my obvious lack of artistic skills. The consensus among the students was that my bananas looked like a cross between a crescent moon and a fingernail, while my professor's mind immediately went to a place that she couldn't share until we were alone.

I tried my best to design bulletin boards that didn't require words to avoid spending *hours* tracing stencils into letters that I would then have to carefully cut out. When packaged, pre-cut letters hit the shelves of teacher supply stores, I felt like I'd won the lottery! And when my school purchased a letter die cut machine, life got even better. Not only could I churn out perfectly formed letters, but I could also create specific shapes and symbols. My room's decor went from chaotically enthusiastic, crooked letters to works of die-cut perfection! At least that's how it felt to me. Every Monday morning, I knew I would need to spend time re-hanging posters on the walls because the masking tape had called it quits over the weekend. When mounting putty came out, it was revolutionary, and I would buy multiple packages at a time, just in case. If I wanted to preserve my classroom posters from year to year, I bought sheets of laminating film. I'd carefully cover my décor, meticulously smoothing each item down until only a few dozen bubbles remained. My mind was blown the first time I saw a laminator in action. I felt as if I'd teleported into the future! (It only took one experience of wrapping the laminator film over the heated roller to make sure I never repeated the mistake.)

Back then, if the air wasn't thick with chalk dust by the time the last bell rang, it wasn't a normal day. Students would jump over one another in their eagerness to go outside to beat erasers against rocks. One year, a parent made me a fancy eraser scraper, which was just a wooden box with chicken wire stretched across the top and nailed down on the edges. I named it Happy, and now my students were even more eager to clean erasers; Happy made me the envy of my hallway. And then I got a job in a brand new, state-of-the-art school. *They had white boards!!* In fact, there were more of them than bulletin boards, which suited me just fine, fancy letter maker or not. The chalk dust was replaced with the scent of dry-erase markers. My lungs improved, but I remember how strange it was the first fall we returned to school without boxes of chalk included in our classroom supplies.

When I first started teaching, playgrounds had tall, steep metal slides whose surfaces could cause burns on a sunny day. They could be rubbed down with waxed paper for a faster ride, which would end in being dumped into a divot that legions of schoolchildren had worn into the ground at the bottom. The twenty-foot-tall rocket climber was standard fare, and kids climbed up to the very top, hanging out the top windows while waving frantically to those far below. Teeter-totters typically came in sets of two, and they were known to catapult friends head over heels if they didn't grip the handles tightly enough. The merry-go-rounds were manned by students who would send them spinning in such fast circles that they became a blur of metal interspersed with glimpses of children's body parts. Those who were unfortunate enough to be catapulted off would brush their scraped knees and get back in line for another turn. Most kids tried their best to hang on because the playground surface was a gooey black asphalt with teeny stones embedded in it. Yet, somehow, few injuries needed care beyond peroxide, mercurochrome, and Band-Aids. (All dispensed by the school secretary, of course!)

One thing that I've been grateful to see change is the strict teacher dress codes that I experienced for the first twenty years of my career. They were not for the faint of heart, and allowed little room for self-expression. Regardless of the grade they were teaching, educators were expected to dress in their Sunday best. It wasn't unusual to see a teacher sitting at her desk, red pen in hand, grading papers with plastic sleeve protectors up to her elbows. Male teachers were required to wear conservative ties that coordinated with their button-down dress shirts, and women didn't even DARE to consider coming to work bare-legged. A female principal once asked if she could feel my calf to make sure I was wearing pantyhose. Today, what I find most amazing is that I didn't think twice before offering up my leg! Indoctrination is real. The strict codes included rules for footwear. All shoes were to be closed-toed, and sneakers were relegated to the once-a-year field day. In 2001, we finally convinced our principal to let us wear open-toed shoes to work. We ambushed him one afternoon in a faculty meeting, pleading our case for wearing sandals in the Georgia heat. He finally relented—as long as we promised to keep our feet and toes well groomed!

Every veteran teacher has experienced having shiny new curricula or programs rolled out every few years. Most often, the new program was almost identical to the curriculum we were already using, just packaged under a different name. And most of the time, those of us in the classroom were already using the "best practices" that the program promised to teach us. America's Choice. Strategic Compensation. Whole Language Reading. Brain Based Learning. Project-Based Learning. Problem-Based Learning. Blended Learning. Experiential Learning. No Child Left Behind. A Nation at Risk. The National Board of Teaching Standards. National Board Certification. Teach for America. Charter schools. Homeschooling. Online schooling. Google Classroom. Back to the Basics. Response to Intervention. Race to the Top. The Common Core. Measures of Academic Progress. Every Student Succeeds. Advanced Placement. International Baccalaureate. The amount of money that is spent on new programs every year is staggering. But in all the decades I've been teaching, I can remember very few times when anyone making the decisions asked what we—the teachers, the ones actually tasked with carrying out the programs—thought. That hasn't changed, in spite of the myriad of initiatives I've watched come and go.

Things change at a relentlessly fast pace, not only in education but in the world. Thank goodness, though, the heart of what teachers do has remained the same. It's said that the more things change, the more they stay the same, and I've watched that play out as students have passed through my doors year after year. In 2003, I was taking a professional development class in which we were required to design the ideal classroom. I wrote that when I told students to take out their notebooks, the "notebooks" would all be computers. The class burst into laughter, me along with them. But just a few short years later, I was teaching in a one-to-one school with an iPad for every student. One year, I was opining to a class of middle school students about how fast technology was evolving. Flipping open my cell phone for emphasis, I said, "I guarantee you, one day these things will be able to access the internet," and, in just a short while, we were all walking around with our noses glued to the screens of our smartphones.

Regardless of whether there's a chalkboard, a whiteboard, or even a Smartboard with all the latest bells and whistles in the front of the room, students need to belong and be seen. That never changes. Whether I'm calculating percentages on a calculator or a computer is doing it for me, what matters most to my students is how I value *them*. All the fancy clothes in the world can't cover up a heart that isn't in the job. Our kids never stop needing a place where they are accepted for who they are. For many, *the classroom is their one safe place*. Child psychologist and educator Haim Ginott wrote, "I've come to a frightening conclusion that I am the decisive element in the classroom. It's my personal approach that creates the climate. . . . As a teacher, I possess a tremendous power to make a child's life miserable or joyous." No matter how things change in the world or in education, the cornerstone will *always* be the relationship between teacher and student. One brick at a time, we build together.

Teaching Tidbit Lesson 1:
They Say the Darndest Things

When you ask a kindergartner who's running a fever and sporting a few blisters on his face if he's ever had the chicken pox, he may say, "No, but I've had a Happy Meal."

If you ever read a book about not saying naughty words like "barf" and "burp" to a group of cute first graders, never ask if students have ever gotten in trouble for using a bad word. Not only will they shock you with their colorful vocabulary, but they will also say the word at the top of their lungs when your community superintendent is walking by.

During the Nancy Reagan "Just Say No to Drugs" era, you may teach your heart out about the geographic zones in your state, fully confident that your fourth-grade students are ready to be evaluated on the information. But you may still get "Drug Free School Zone" on the question that asks what zone we live in. And you may give them credit anyway.

If a student tells you that his mom stays in bed all day for her job, take him at his word. Don't ask for more information.

When it's time for standardized testing and your third graders are jittery, one of them might burst into tears when you give them a pencil for the test because it says "No 2."

When a kindergartner's mom is late picking her up, the student may tell you she's worried that her mom had a "nervous wreck."

Sometimes students whose first language is not English say cute things. It seems learning a new language isn't a "pizza cake."

Some years age you so quickly that a kindergarten student may look at the ID hanging around your neck and tell you that the picture must have been taken when you were MUCH younger. You know, the picture that was taken during the first week of school. Four months ago.

When a first grader tells you that his mother is a virgin, you may learn that she doesn't eat vegetables.

When one of your second graders tells you that his mom got a "stimulated" diamond ring for Christmas, you just let it go.

You may work very hard with a particular fifth grader, helping him memorize portions of a speech by Dr. Martin Luther King, Jr. And on the night of the performance, in front of a packed audience, his nerves may get the best of him and instead of "Protestants and Catholics" he may instead say "Prostitutes and Catholics."

During a vocabulary lesson focusing on long vowels, a student may continually read the words as if they have short vowels instead. When you ask him why he can't remember that he's working on words with the long vowel sound, he may say, "I guess I have short-term memory loss."

Chapter 4

A Lifetime to Pay It Forward

By the time I started school, I was a needy little girl who craved affection and acceptance. My small town was served by three schools: one elementary, one middle, and one high. Each of those buildings housed some of the most gifted educators I've ever known. There was Mrs. May, my first-grade teacher, who ignited a love of learning in me that has never stopped. I remember the moment when words began to make sense as the magic of learning to read took hold. I'd read anything I could—the milk carton, the bathroom walls, and the comics. My parents finally banned me from reading billboards as we drove down the road because of my incessant chatter. Mrs. May just had a knack for teaching her students to love reading. She chose a "Star Student" each week, and I spent weeks working so hard to earn the title. For a six-year-old-girl, the week that MY name went up on the board was better than winning an Olympic gold medal. Five decades later, I can recall putting my head on my desk and peeking out from between my arms as Mrs. May erased the previous week's winner, hoping with my entire being that I'd see my name being neatly spelled out in white chalk.

Mrs. Ware was my third-grade math teacher, but she taught me much more than the times tables. She was a loving model of quiet calm, and her weekly reading of Mark Twain's *The Adventures of Tom Sawyer* to the entire grade was the highlight of every week.

Aunt Polly's exasperation with Tom's escapades, Huckleberry Finn's independent life, and Becky Thatcher's braids were as real to me as the person sitting next to me on the cold tile floor.

My report cards consistently noted that I needed to work on my handwriting and curb my tendency to talk incessantly, and fifth grade was no exception. One day, my teacher, Mrs. Hill, left the room and covertly turned on a cassette tape recorder to see if we'd adhere to her admonition to work on our math and be silent until she returned. Since I hadn't liked math since Mrs. Ware's third-grade class, I chose to socialize instead of doing my work. I was so embarrassed when, upon her return, Mrs. Hill played the tape back, hearing only one very chatty voice on the tape—mine. That was not the first or the last time my socializing landed me in hot water with her, and there were always consequences. But this was one of the first times I understood that I could do something wrong and still be valued and seen. I have no memory of Mrs. Hill's math lessons, but the *life* lessons of unconditional acceptance were unforgettable.

My sixth-grade PE teacher, Mrs. Brunson, always took time to check in with me daily, and she became my go-to person whenever I was hurting. Whether it was girl drama with my friends, exasperation with my parents, or seeing the first C on my report card (math, of course), Mrs. Brunson was always there. She also encouraged my love of writing, especially poetry. I'd compose endless verses, write story after story, and each time I shared one of my masterpieces with her, she made me feel like the next Emily Dickinson. For years afterward, Mrs. Brunson's continued presence in my life helped mitigate a lot of my teenage angst and turbulence. Her example of unconditional love has stayed with me my entire life.

My high school history teacher, Mrs. Grant, never failed to make time for me when I needed to vent. Whether it was relationship drama or turmoil at home, she always listened and never failed to check in with me after a particularly rough day. Mrs. Grant's sweet, gentle, nonjudgmental attitude was a model for the teacher I hope I have been for my own students.

Ms. Garrard taught English at my high school, although I was never enrolled in her class. But from the moment I unintentionally wandered into her room one day after school, she became an instant source of support. When my thirty-six-year-old mother was diagnosed with cancer my junior year, Ms. Garrard became a rock in the middle of the turbulence. She introduced me to her sister-in-law, who'd lost her own mother as a teenager. Although I was emotionally devastated, I was absolutely secure in the love of those two women, and seeing myself through Ms. Garrard's eyes gave me hope that I'd be okay someday.

The months of my mom's illness were some of the darkest times I've ever known. An experience with Mrs. Marshall, my high school math teacher, exemplifies how my teachers supported me. After four months of sickness, my young mother died on a cold February morning. The days that followed were a blur, but I remember seeing teachers from elementary, middle, and high school at the funeral service. When the last person left our house after the funeral, I picked up the newspaper and went to Mom's room to read. Huddled between the bed and the wall, I immediately turned to the obituary section. It seemed surreal to be reading my own mother's death notice and seeing my name listed as a survivor. It suddenly became very real, and I read the obituary over and over, weeping over the words. In the quiet of that bedroom, I began to understand that my family's life was irrevocably changed.

As I lay on the floor, curled into a ball, and cried, a quiet knock sounded on the door. I was in no shape to talk to anyone, but Mrs. Marshall didn't wait for me to answer. She just came in, and, spotting me curled up on the floor, she didn't say a word. She simply walked across the room, sat down beside me and took me in her arms, and held me. Neither of us spoke for a long time, but words weren't necessary. Mrs. Marshall's actions spoke louder than anything she could have uttered. She had two young children at home and lived over a half-hour away, yet she'd made the time to come and be with me at the time when I needed it most. I was a lousy math student. I didn't enjoy it, didn't understand it, and definitely didn't make Mrs. Marshall feel successful when I struggled through a geometry theorem. But I was more to her than a score on an evaluation at the end of the year. She saw me as a person first, and that influenced my life more than any high score on an exam, before or since.

As you can imagine, the months after Mom died were a huge adjustment for my entire family. As the oldest of three, I suddenly found myself responsible for grocery shopping for our now family of four. Ms. Garrard didn't wait to be asked for help. One day, she loaded me up in her El Camino and took me on my first shopping excursion. She showed me how to pick out the best fruit and check expiration dates. She helped me compare prices and ingredients. In the spring, she took me shopping for a prom dress with funds that had been collected by the community for just that purpose. That summer, several teachers took me on vacation with their families. I dove from docks into a lake and jumped ocean waves with their children. And my sixteen-year-old heart began to slowly heal. During my college years, I spent weekends and holidays in their homes. For years afterward, they opened their homes whenever I needed a place to stay.

A few years ago, I wrote to each of these teachers and told them that I'd begun to speak to audiences about how their influence had shaped the person I became. I told them of the ripple effect that was happening with my own students as I followed in their footsteps. It meant the world to me to see how much it touched all of them, and a note from Mrs. Grant sums up their responses: "Teaching is a key to immortality, for those you touch will touch others through the generations. I remember you so vividly, the broken-hearted girl in the eleventh grade. I loved you then, and I love you even more now." I've spent my life since paying forward what those women did for me, but I'll never come close to paying off the debt. These real teachers changed the world for me.

I Am

I am practical and kind
I wonder often what I will be when I grow up
I hear the rushing waterfall from my deck that helps calm my
rambling thoughts
I see the amazing beauty God has created all around me
I want the Georgia Dawgs to have a winning season every year
I am practical and fun.
I pretend in my tinnitus buzzing head that I am still young
I feel love and acceptance when holding my grands tight in my
arms
I touch my heart to help my anxious mind feel at peace
I wonder if I have always set a good example according to my
parents' wishes
I cry easily since I am so emotional over happy and sad movies
and events in my life
I am practical and fun.
I understand that life is hard and tough and that is what makes
us stronger
I say to friends, Let's get together when we can - lunch, bridge,
and girls' trips make us better
I dream about special memories from my past and hope to make
more before I pass
I try to stay positive and look for the best in every situation
I hope and pray for a happy and bright future for my children
and grandchildren
I am practical and fun.

-Kay Hill, Lisa's fifth grade teacher

I Am

I am empathetic and hard-working.
I wonder why teachers are not valued far more than media
celebrities and sports figures in both respect and monetary
remunerations.
I hear a ringing sound when I feel guilt or shame.
I see an image of myself twenty years younger when I look in my
"magical" bathroom mirror.
I want people to stop quarreling and to start listening to each
other with tolerance and respect for differences of opinion.
I am empathetic and hard-working.
I pretend to be fine when I am quite the opposite.
I feel the touch of my late husband's hand caress my cheek.
I touch the luxuriant fur of my beloved departed cat.
I worry over the health and viability of our physical world.
I cry over the hatred, injustice, and lack of tolerance so blatantly
revealed every day in the news.
I am empathetic and hard-working.
I understand how short even a long life can be.
I say love God above all and love our neighbors as we love
ourselves.
I dream that I am thin and beautiful even as I eat all I want of
my favorite foods.
I hope to see my grandchildren develop into happy and produc-
tive adults.
I am empathetic and hard-working.

-Evelyn Grant, Lisa's high school history teacher

I Am

I am loud and proud
I wonder what's around the next curve and over the next hill I
hear cries of anguish, peals of laughter, never silence I see the
promise of tomorrow in a child's smile I want to share love, hap-
piness, and the joy of being alive I am loud and proud
I pretend that everything will be manageable
I feel like the luckiest person ever
I touch moonlight, sunbeams, and wind
I worry that human indifference will destroy our fragile Earth
I cry because of people's inhumanity
I am loud and proud
I understand that the world needs love
I say it is better to be seen than viewed
I dream of strolling by Scottish lochs and climbing Irish
mountains
I try to be happy and positive every day
I hope to see my grandchildren as young adults I am loud and
proud.

-M J Garrard, Lisa's high school support teacher

Chapter 5

Back from the Edge

Even with the support of those who loved me, my late teens and early twenties were incredibly difficult, and I was nearly crippled by debilitating depression. By the time I started teaching, I was a mess, both emotionally and physically. In 1987, I was hired to teach second grade in a tiny rural community in northeast Georgia. The school had burned down fifteen years before, and my classroom was housed in the old cafeteria, which hadn't burned because it wasn't attached to the school. It was old and musty, but to me, it was the most beautiful building I'd ever seen. Most days were still a fight, and getting out of bed was usually a huge struggle. But I knew if I could make it to my classroom, I'd be okay because the blackness somehow never penetrated the walls. I wasn't a perfect teacher, and those children weren't always model students, but I was the best version of myself when I was there with them. On the weekends, I'd often drive the thirty miles to my classroom, ostensibly to work. But the truth was, it was my safe place.

That January, after a panicked drive to the hospital after school one day, I found myself undergoing emergency surgery for a tear in my stomach wall. As they were prepping me for surgery, I was frantically scribbling emergency lesson plans on a hospital menu. (If you're a teacher, you totally understand.) The medical staff finally took it out of my hands when the anesthesiologist arrived to take me to happy land. Afterward, I had to take a few weeks off to heal, but I was back in the classroom as soon as possible. Those children were the medicine I most needed. I could have never imagined how much I'd miss my students, my classroom—my home. This was when I began to understand and appreciate just how much I *needed* teaching. Those sweet children gave me so much.

Talk about coming full circle. First, teachers saved me, and later, teaching did the same. Gradually, the depression began to lose its tenacious grip, and eventually, the blackness of those early years became a memory. And while I was blessed with amazing mental health support, it was teaching that truly pulled me back from the edge. Over the years, the same fulfillment I found in the classroom infiltrated other areas of my life, but it all began in an old converted school cafeteria. It still amazes me. And my gratitude is unlimited.

The decades have passed, and although the schools, faces, grade levels, and even states have changed, the one constant has been the way my life has been continually shaped and changed by my students, my tribe, my people. Teaching is so much more than a profession. It is even more than a calling. It is our chance to leave something greater than ourselves behind. It is life changing.

I'm *living* proof.

I Am

I am introverted and shy
I wonder what the future will bring
I hear everyone I've lost
I see colors when listening to music
I want to be proud of who I am
I am introverted and shy.

I pretend that I'm like everyone else
I feel like anything is possible
I touch the lives of others
I worry about when I'll have another panic attack
I cry when I think of my past
I am introverted and shy.

I understand that everyone has different needs
I say that I know what I'm doing
I dream that my future will be bright
I try to keep moving forward
I hope that I'll see my brother again
I am introverted and shy.

—Elizabeth, age fifteen

Chapter 6

CommUNITY

I'd be willing to bet that for the vast majority of us, when we think back to our years in school, it's not the knowledge gained that first comes to mind. We are, first and foremost, social creatures, and we yearn for meaningful, rich relationships. Feeling connected to others is a deep, basic human need. Novelist and family therapist Chris Crutcher wrote, "I know very little having to do with human beings that doesn't also have to do with human connection." I believe that the desire for connection is so strong that we connect with whatever is available. Addiction has been called the "disease of disconnection," and connecting with others is ultimately what brings people back from the isolation of addiction. From my first day of teaching, I was driven to create an atmosphere of belonging in my classroom. Over the years, I've called it many different names—our family, our tribe, our team. Regardless of the name, the theme was the same—there is a place for everyone here; we all belong within that classroom space.

I've taught in areas where gangs were very prevalent in the school and community. Students who were members of the gangs would tell me how the group provided a family for them, in spite of the negatives that came with the association. It gave them a place to belong. The power of playing for a sports team has less to do with the win/loss record than with being a member of a community. Kids form support groups that are centered around music, drama, art, debate—the list goes on and on. Over the years, colleagues have asked me about how I form such a strong unit with my students, and it's hard to explain. I think that my own deep need to belong when I was growing up has been the driving force. It's always been such a central part of my story.

I'm very aware that many of my readers are skilled at creating community. Hopefully I don't come across as if I believe I am the only educator that works to create connections with students. I just believe in helping students feel visible, needed, and valued. Have you ever seen one of Steve Spangler's energy sticks? They are so sensitive that they can detect even a very small amount of electricity in the skin. However, they only light up when a circuit is completed. Holding just one end doesn't make it light up, but when two people each grab an end of the tube, watch out! The tube springs to vibrant life, illustrating the forces between objects (people) and the changes in energy due to the interaction. This visual representation is a powerful reminder of how we as humans complete one another, and I love using it as a way to demonstrate to my students how important and necessary we all are to each other.

I've always tried to make sure the classroom looked like it belonged to all of us. Before the fire marshal put an end to it, students would decorate the ceiling tiles in my classrooms. Sometimes, the art was curriculum related, and sometimes, it consisted of quotes students chose that represented them. Colleagues of mine have escaped the scrutiny of the authorities year after year, and their decorated ceiling tiles have stayed up, which makes me jealous! Students' artwork adorned the walls of my classroom, and they loved to come back in later years to see their younger selves portrayed in living color. Whether it was in the form of murals or specific quotes they had chosen, they had a part in creating our classroom home. When we ran out of space on the walls, we painted canvases—anything to make the room truly reflect everyone who was a part of our class.

Joy is a great example of the power that comes from these simple acts. The week before our annual mural painting extravaganza was to commence, I was sitting on one of our large over-stuffed couches grading papers. Joy plopped down beside me, eyes filled with tears. She told me she had yet to decide on the quote she wanted to paint, and as the tears fell harder and faster, she was able to choke out that her grandpa had died a few months before, right before she started high school. Joy went on to tell me about the special relationship they'd shared and how much she continued to grieve his loss. Although she was unsure whether it would be appropriate, she wanted to use one of her grandpa's original quotes. I reminded Joy that I *expect* my students to follow their hearts, that the space belongs to them, not me. Soon, she was telling me stories about her grandpa, bringing him to life, smiles beginning to replace the tears. I told her it would be an honor to have his words live in our room as a testament to a life well-lived. A few weeks later, her family came by after school one afternoon to see Joy's completed masterpiece, including Grandma, who had said goodbye to her husband just a few months before. Watching them read the quote as they gently ran their fingers over the words with tears in their eyes was so moving!

One day, after years of changing out bulletin boards, I was done, so I decided to turn my five-mile-long board (okay, maybe that's a bit of hyperbole; it took FOREVER to get that thing filled up) into something I called our "Community Bulletin Board." It underwent several iterations, but regardless of the theme, it was a place for students to share thoughts with their peers. I divided it into class periods, put a class roster in each section so everyone would know where to leave messages, and left a basket of sticky notes with a stapler on a nearby table. A few students in each class acted as monitors, and kept up with who was getting messages, and they would write notes to students who weren't getting many notes.

During holidays, the kids turned the board into a celebration. Students would bring in little trinkets and snacks related to the time of year, and it never got old seeing faces light up when students spotted their name on a little treat. I also got creative with the board itself. When we took the background paper down to design a new board, it might be several days or more before we got new paper up. We painted the entire bulletin board black, and then students used silver and gold Sharpies to write quotes and positive messages. That way, even if there was no bulletin board to interact with at the moment, there was something positive, uplifting, and supportive in place.

On the first day of school, regardless of the grade, I focused on getting to know my new class. I created interest inventories that were as creative and interesting as I could make them. I'd ask about the most important people in their lives and what made those people so special. Collections, favorite *everything*—music, color, movie, person, number, animal, snack food—so many things made the list. When a student hit a rough patch, accomplished something special, or if I felt they just needed a boost, I'd already have a list of their personal favorites available. I included things on the inventory such as "Most people think I'm _____, but really, I'm _____." One favorite question for me was "How would your parents describe you versus your friends and peers?"

For those students who weren't able to write well, due to age or language, for example, I'd interview them rather than give them the paper directly. Once all of my students had more access to technology, I'd have them create slides about themselves that we'd turn into a presentation called "All about Our Tribe." Sometimes, I'd expand this into a project inspired by a colleague that I called "Playlist of My Life." Students chose music that represented them, with a minimum number of songs required. They'd present their list, explaining how each song related to them personally. I created a playlist of my own that I showed at the beginning of the year, giving my kids the chance to know me on a deeper level.

In addition to our personal playlists, I'd have each student tell me a few of their favorite songs, and as long as the lyrics wouldn't get me fired, I created a class playlist. I loved playing their music during interludes when they were working independently.

I also assigned parent inventories. At the start of the school year, I'd send home a document that asked questions such as *What do you most love about your child?*, *What do you imagine your child will be doing in the future?*, *What would you like to see your child work to improve?*, and *What makes your child unique?*

It was amazing how much I could learn about my students from their parents' perspectives! It also helped remind me that every single one of those kids sitting in my room day after day was not just a student, but also someone's child.

Having a class nickname was always a hit. Lee's Zoo Crew, LL's Cool J's, The Room 13 Tribe, K-9 Krazys, The Doghouse, and The Village People are some that I've used over the years. One year, we created our own Hogwarts House, FeatherWing. We'd choose class colors, create a mascot, and sometimes even decorate t-shirts to represent our "team". Masking tape letters painted over with spray paint look *almost* professional when you pull the tape off.

I've always made a point for students to welcome one another back from an absence so they would know that they had been missed. Knowing that our classroom was the one place where some students felt safe and accepted, I believed it was so important that when they missed school, their absence was noticed.

Like most of my colleagues when I taught elementary school, I had a space in my classroom to display student birthdays, but I didn't put it up in my middle school classroom. One day, a seventh grader came into class so excited that it was her birthday. It made me question why I had assumed that these "big kids" were too old for birthday displays. The next day when students came to class, I had put up a birthday train, the very same one I'd used with my kindergartners. Those kids were thrilled to see their birthdays listed on the train cars.

Another way I've tried to form a close community is by paying attention to my language. I don't mean making sure I didn't use curse words (that ship sailed a long time ago, anyway), but I am careful with the terms I casually use when referring to students. At the age of sixteen, when I suddenly found myself motherless, it seemed that *everyone* around me, regardless of age, seemed to have a nuclear family unit. When I'd fill out forms for various activities and there was a place for "mother's name," it always pierced my heart. Even in conversations, it seemed to be a given—tell your parents this or that; ask your mom. I realize that this happened to me at a very vulnerable age, but I've never forgotten the power of those words and how they made me feel. Today I find myself raising a pair of grandtwins, and they have talked about how left out they feel when someone says, "Tell your mom," "Ask your dad," "Tell your parents about . . ."

The family unit has changed so much over the course of my career, but our society hasn't evolved with its vocabulary concerning family relationships. I don't believe the lack of responsiveness is the result of not caring about others' lives. When my fourth-grade grandson was taking guitar lessons as part of an after-school enrichment program, the registration form asked for "Dad's name" and "Mom's name" and even included sections for "Dad's cell phone" and "Mom's cell phone", I wrote an email to the organization that sponsors the guitar lessons, asking if they might consider changing their wording to make it more inclusive. I received an email back from the program director. She shared she had just been talking about rewording the form with her coworker. In addition, she asked for my input because she had "been in the education arena before parent/guardian, grandparents, or two same-sex parents became more prevalent." The director ended with questions about how to ask for the information without ignoring or offending anyone.

I have so much appreciation for those who are mindful of children who don't come from what our society has idealized as a "normal" family. The next time your school or organization considers having a "Daddy-Daughter Dance" or a "Muffins for Moms" breakfast, think about ways to make them sound more inclusive.

Instead of using terms like "Tell your parents" and "Ask your mom and dad," I have friends who use "Tell your grownups" and "Ask your parents or guardians" instead. When you're making presents and cards for Mother's Day, remember that there are others raising children who fill that role but don't have the title. It's not a situation of being politically correct, but one of being compassionate and considerate toward all of those we teach.

Teaching Tidbit Lesson 2:
Not for the Faint of Heart

When a student comes to tell you that the bag of popcorn you shoved into the microwave before heading out to hall duty is on fire, don't dismiss it as eighth-grade hyperbole. Especially if there's a snowstorm outside. Especially, *especially,* if the totally hot firefighters don't have a sense of humor.

When using fog machines for dramatic effect on Halloween, you may discover that they can set off the fire alarm. And firefighters don't like that either.

You will encounter a lot of vomit, and most of it will be outside of the bathroom. In the classroom. On the playground. On the bus. In the cafeteria. A lot of vomit.

If you have couches in your high school classroom, make sure the doors are locked when you leave for the day. Use your imagination. Or don't.

When teaching ANY grade, never, ever, ever touch unknown substances and ask, "What is this?" And if you do, try not to do it more than once. Or twice. I cannot stress this enough.

If a kindergarten student's shoelaces are wet when you help tie them, just pretend it never happened.

When a freshman asks if he can build a potato mortar for his fall project and you say yes, it may turn out to be a pneumatic cannon, a.k.a. a pipe bomb. You realize this when his parents bring it to school to demonstrate and the missile lands blocks away.

I Am

I am silly and smart.
I wonder if there is going to be an earthquake magnitude 20?
I hear words and melodies of the wind
I see an astronaut falling from the sky
I want my mom, my dad, and my brother to live long
I am silly and smart.

I pretend to be brave when I'm scared
I feel like I'm running as fast as a car
I touch zombies in their face
I worry about tsetse flies, earthquakes, asteroids, and my family
dying
I cry when I have a bad dream
I am silly and smart.

I understand that there are words and memories
I say a zombie apocalypse can happen
I dream about my dad stopping being pre-diabetic
I try really hard at solving impossible multiplication problems
I hope for the world to be in balance
I am silly and smart.

Nick, age seven

Chapter 7

From Country to City

After completing my inaugural year of teaching, I traded in small-town life for the big city. This is when I found myself working in an inner-city elementary school, so different from the bucolic farming community I'd left behind. This community was composed mostly of families who lived an almost day-to-day existence, something I couldn't relate to. I had never experienced hunger, never gone without having a roof over my head, never had to scramble to get my basic needs met. Although I didn't grow up in an affluent family, we never lacked for what we needed. The expectation of having children arrive in my classroom well nourished, rested, and ready to learn was no longer viable. When I had to ask a child who'd been awake all night because he was hungry to perform well on a standardized test, it felt cruel.

Literacy rates in the community were low, crime was high, drug use was rampant, and student retention rates were off the charts. There were no limits to how many times a student could be "held back," and it wasn't unusual to have fourteen-year-olds passing pre-K children in the hallways. On Mondays, children would come in and tell us about the automatic weapons they'd spied on their way to school, ditched as a result of weekend police raids when things had to be gotten rid of quickly. Often, a gun would wind up under one of the school's mobile classrooms or under a piece of playground equipment. One of my kindergartners once found a packet of cocaine in our housekeeping center, nestled inside the cabinet of a miniature kitchen set. She brought it to me, correctly identifying the white powder, and I was floored that the kids could tell me the value of the baggie. Suffice it to say that kids grew up fast in that community.

In the seven years I spent at this school, I was forged in fire. I came out a different person than the one who walked in for her interview dressed in pearls, a lacy cream silk blouse, an electric blue linen skirt, and shiny black heels. The faculty and staff became as close as family, and well over thirty years later, they remain among my closest friends and adopted family. Together, we wrote lesson plans, drove children to dentists, constructed Thanksgiving baskets, and wrapped and delivered Christmas presents we'd gathered for the community. But most of all, *we loved those kids.*

Not long after starting my career there, I came to a startling realization that was difficult to admit, even to myself. *Especially* to myself. I discovered I believed poor people didn't love their children as much as those who were more financially blessed. I'm embarrassed to even write those words, but it was something that had somehow taken root. Whether through messages from the media, beliefs I'd unknowingly acquired while growing up, or just the fact that I'd never taken the time to look below the surface of families living in poverty, I had a lot of growing to do. Although I'd never verbalized those beliefs to anyone, even to myself, I quickly realized that they had operated underneath my awareness. And those beliefs were absolutely wrong. I had a lot to learn.

When parents came to pick their children up on Friday afternoons, I saw them cry because they didn't have enough to eat for the weekend. Single mothers would tell me stories of how they'd hover over their children in darkened rooms while gangs exchanged gunfire right outside their door. I watched families who couldn't afford recreational sports show up to play baseball and soccer with their children on the school fields. You know how the Grinch's heart "grew three times that day"? That's how my awareness grew while teaching at that inner-city school, although it didn't happen that quickly. I gradually grew to realize that there was a big difference between physical poverty and emotional poverty. The love that these families had for their children was every bit as rich and deep as any I'd ever seen or known. I can't imagine the pain they felt knowing they were unable to provide for their well-loved children like they wished they could. And I learned that the cycle of poverty is real, and it has nothing to do with the value or quality of the humans who exist within it.

But even though the environment was intense, so was the enjoyment. Every day was an adventure, and whenever a group of us gather to reminisce about those days, we have such stories to tell! For example, let me tell you about Quentin—one of my first graders who earned the chance to come decorate cookies at my apartment with all the students in my class who'd improved their grades. We had such fun decorating, dancing, and singing, and before I knew it, friends who had volunteered to come help drive kids home arrived and we headed out. I chose to take the group of kids who lived in the neighborhood's most dangerous apartment complex. In fact, the word dangerous doesn't even scratch the surface of the things that happened in that neighborhood. The police wouldn't go into the area without a partner, and they periodically came to school to talk to the faculty and staff about staying out of the area if at all possible.

With my typical bravado, I loaded the kids into my little white Nissan Sentra and headed out into the dark night, giving myself silent pep talks as I drove. As soon as we pulled into the poorly lit complex, Quentin said in his distinctive, gravelly voice, "They KILL people in my neighborhood! We hear guns ALL NIGHT LONG. And they always look for white people to shoot!" He seemed to be oblivious to the fact that a white woman was at the wheel, and I began to slink down into the seat, eventually sliding down so far I could could barely peep above the dash of the car to see where

I was going. Yet even though that story makes me laugh, and I can still remember the in-over-my-head feeling that hit me when I pulled up to Quentin's apartments, it served as a reminder of the environment my kids lived in. Extension cords snaked from one window to another so that residents could share power, and nearly every building was tagged with gang graffiti. It was their daily existence—those living in the apartments couldn't drive away in a little white Nissan like I could. (And, I must say, I did so very quickly!)

Ms. Williams is a great example of the love that the families living in these challenging conditions had for one another. Ms. Williams had three children who were all enrolled at the school. She suffered from a mental condition that was *mostly* controlled if she took her medicine, but she was known to skip it. A lot. Those were memorable days. I have memories of her sitting on the bench at the school's entrance with a bucket of KFC between her legs, wearing a short dress with nothing underneath. She'd wave a drumstick around in the air and pontificate about life to anyone passing by.

One year, her youngest son had to go to a disciplinary hearing at the district's administration building, a serious event run very much like a formal trial. Mrs. Chandler, the school's beloved secretary, was someone Ms. Williams leaned on for advice and used as her personal ATM. (She always paid her back on the first of the month.) Mrs. Chandler had been subpoenaed to testify as a witness at the disciplinary hearing. When Mrs. Chandler took the witness stand and Mrs. Williams evidently felt that the district's attorneys were not treating her with the respect that Mrs. Williams felt Mrs. Chandler deserved, she jumped up and began yelling at everyone present, ranting that they needed to leave Mrs. Chandler alone, that she was a GOOD person, and that she herself would come after them if they kept it up. Somehow, everyone emerged from that hearing without being arrested, including Mrs. Williams and her son, and another story was born.

One year, I was teaching kindergarten when I heard the teacher across the hall shriek, "WHAT ARE YOU DOING?!" I hurried over to see if I was needed, and although I don't know what I expected to find, it certainly wasn't one of her kindergartners who'd magically sprouted a mustache. He'd equipped himself with glue, scissors, and . . . the hair of the little girl who sat next to him. The little girl now sported a bald spot on the back of her head, and the formerly clean-shaven student was proudly showing off thick facial hair dripping with Elmer's glue.

While we're on the subject of mustaches, another story comes to mind. I began teaching at this school in March, taking over for a beloved fourth-grade teacher who'd gotten a job as a counselor at another school in the district. She and I had very different teaching styles, and I guess I didn't measure up. Those students made it their mission in life to punish me for Mother Teresa's, I mean their revered teacher's, departure. Although this was only year two of my career, I honestly felt like I'd lost every smidgen of teaching ability I'd ever had. I'd survived a petition to remove me in order to bring our school's Mother Teresa back, and I had also lived through the classroom lights crashing down because students were using them for chin-ups during class, so I was hardly fazed the day one of the boys grabbed a bottle of Wite-Out and gave anyone who wished a swirly handlebar mustache.

When they began to complain about the way their new facial hair stung, begging to go to the bathroom to wash it off, I refused until the end of class. And, of course, *that's* when the principal walked in to do a formal observation. You just can't make this stuff up. Years later, I went through the drive-thru at a nearby McDonald's to get a drink. I scrounged around for change while I was waiting for my soda and finally turned to the window with my hand outstretched. Staring at me through that drive-thru window was one of the fourth-grade students who'd most terrorized me that year. I guess my face gave away my feelings because she just looked at me and slowly nodded her head up and down several times without saying a word. As soon as I was out of sight, I opened my car door and poured every drop of my Diet Coke out. I never returned to that particular restaurant, even though it was much more convenient than the one I started going to afterwards. Maybe it was my imagination, or just pure terror at the flashbacks I had when I got to that drive-thru window, but I swear her eyes were glowing red. And shooting sparks.

The next year, I started out with a new crop of students who were "mine" from the start, and my confidence and love of teaching came storming back. On November 9, 1989, the Berlin Wall fell. To these fourth graders sitting in that inner-city neighborhood, that historic event might as well have been happening on Mars. The morning after the German people began to tear the wall down, I got to school three hours early. I strung a wire down the middle of the classroom, flung sheets over it, and designated one side East Germany and the other West. When students came in, they were assigned to sit on one side of the wall. West Germans enjoyed a morning of choice. They could decide which assignments to complete, what activities to participate in during PE, and what to eat for lunch. East Germans were given orders and directives from the moment they walked in the door. There was no choice, no room for individualism, no tolerance for dissension. They were issued three "tokens" for the day, which were to be used for things West Germans could do whenever they liked, such as sharpening a pencil or borrowing a piece of paper. At no time were the two sides allowed to communicate. Halfway through the day, the students changed sides so that everyone had the experience of living in both regions.

At the end of the day, we all tore the wall down. There were cheers and tears. The rejoicing was heartfelt and raucous. These events happened long before our buildings had computers and the internet, before I came to rely on my Smartboard for every lesson, and if we wanted to look up information, we headed to the Encyclopedia Britannica. Back when education was not a plank on a candidate's political platform, when standardized tests were just one small measurement of a student's progress and a teacher's proficiency, there was an innocence to teaching that I miss. I feel so blessed to have lived and taught in such times.

I'd been teaching at this school for two years when we got a new principal. Bill was kind, funny, and totally green. It wasn't long before he realized how big his learning curve was going to be, but we loved him, and he is still a treasured part of my life. That fall, one of our fifth-grade students was murdered by a former student on her way to school. Can you imagine being a new principal and having *that* as part of your baptism by fire? I remember that I was completely outraged when this happened. For years, teachers had been trying to get someone to intervene with this family, but no actions were ever taken, as far as any of us could see. Long before the tragedy, we all felt like our concerns fell on deaf ears, and although our school came together to help with funeral expenses and to support the family, I knew we'd failed her. The child never got the support and intervention she deserved, and I believe it made her an easy target.

A few years later, I had the sister of the convicted murderer in my first-grade class. As you can imagine, the family had been through a great deal of trauma over the years, and one day, the mother asked for a conference. In tears, she begged me to take her daughter in and raise her as my own because she was just too overwhelmed to parent anymore. My own life circumstances weren't in a place where I could step up as I'd have liked to, and to this day, I wonder what became of that sweet little girl and her desperate mom.

So many memories are centered around that brick-and-mortar building. Whether it is my newly hatched duckling, Ali Goose Jemima Puddleduck, following me through the halls with a matching bandanna, or the secretary panicking when she walked by my room and saw me sprawled out on the floor (everyone had brought their homework that morning, and I "fainted" from the "shock"), or the endless stories that were lived out in front of me every day, this school completely shaped me into the educator I am today. Title I schools have a teacher turnover rate of more than 50 percent! It is hard work, and I personally feel that educators in those schools need to be paid more. Since that time, I've taught in several other Title I schools, and the lessons learned, as well as the relationships that emerged, remain central to my life. It was in this environment that I believe my own identity as a "real teacher" began to emerge. In the midst of the challenges that no college of education or professional development course could have prepared me for, I *thrived*. When those kids walked into the building, an invisible safety net descended, and we entered a world in which minds could expand, hearts could heal, and teachers and students could learn and grow together.

Teaching Tidbit Lesson 3:
What's in a Name?

Someday you might teach three adorable little second graders whose names are pronounced "Me," "You," and "We" in the same class. And when you say, "We need to be quiet," it turns into an argument of "But I'm not talking," followed by, "She's not talking to You, she's talking to Me," which of course is followed by, "She's not talking to Me, she's talking to You!" You might feel as if you're living out a true-life version of Abbott and Costello's "Who's on First" every single day.

A first grader might be stunned that you figured out she copied her friend's math worksheet. You let her think you're all seeing and all knowing, but you secretly giggle because she also copied her friend's name.

It's possible to teach a sibling group named Faith, Hope, and ...Charlie.

If you have two Roberts in the same seventh-grade class, you might give them nicknames in order to distinguish them. At parent-teacher conferences, as the teachers on your team are sharing their nicknames for the pair with the mother of the most mischievous of the two Roberts, when it's your turn you may blurt out "Little S*#@" before you realize you've even opened your mouth. You and the mom will subsequently become best buds.

When two of your kindergarten students have talked continually about their family, "Fat Daddy" figuring prominently in their conversations, and you drive them home late in the school year, you may discover that "Fat Daddy" is a four-year-old sibling, not a bachelor uncle.

Sometimes, a fifth-grade boy whose family has limited English might wear a t-shirt to school that says "bride."

Someday, you may ask a kindergartner if she knows her mom's first name. If she says no, you may ask, "What does your daddy call her?" When she answers, "Darlin'," you will want to nominate them for Family of the Year.

If you ever teach a sister and brother pair in first grade whose names are Phuc and Phu. be very careful to pronounce the "u" as "oo," as in "choose." Their parents did not. When their mom arrives at your classroom door every afternoon to pick them up, she will always say, "I am here to pick up Phuc and Phu." (Say it fast. In your head.) It will never get old.

You may get an email from sexkitten69. Don't delete it. It may be the parent of one of your seventh-grade students.

Someday you may meet a new student named Heaven. When you jokingly ask her if she's an angel, she may say, "No. That's my sister."

And, in the "I'm not Clever Enough to Make this Up":
It's possible to teach April, Summer, Autumn, and Snow in one class.
It's also possible to have a kindergarten class with the last names of Blue, Brown, Green, and White.

Although it isn't pronounced like the GI issue, your student whose name is spelled Dyaria will indeed be a little *^%!.

Chapter 8

Politically Speaking

It was 2008, an election year, and I was teaching seventh- and eighth-grade social studies. The McCain/Obama campaign was in full swing, and given the historical significance of the election, I decided to design a unit that took us from the beginning of a presidential campaign all the way through to Inauguration Day. Regardless of political leanings, we knew we were living history. Since I had to cover other grade-level standards in addition to the election unit, the unit stretched out for several months. We worked on it a few days each week, and students stayed engaged the entire time.

Just as with the actual campaigns, we started with a caucus to determine which candidates would move forward. The debates were spirited and engaging as students became familiar with the platforms of their preferred candidates. They wrote impassioned speeches, vigorously waved posters they'd covered with original slogans when someone spoke in favor of their candidate, and fact-checked one another. Quite a few were surprised to find the arguments of their peers so compelling that they actually changed candidates! Once the final candidates were selected, they began to campaign hard. Several parents told me that their children were better informed on the issues than they themselves were. The results mirrored what was actually happening in the nation, although in our version, Hillary Clinton came very close to edging out Barack Obama. Students hung posters all over the school, wrote announcements to be included in school correspondence, and once a week, they were allowed to give a pitch for their candidate during morning announcements.

We held miniature versions of the Republican and Democratic National Conventions. Heartfelt speeches were given, culminating in celebrations as each party moved its candidate forward. We followed McCain and Obama on the campaign trail, convening each week to discuss the most recent developments for each party. We not only watched and discussed the presidential debates, but held our own as well. As a longtime voter, I've never felt more in tune with a campaign than I did during that year.

When Election Day finally arrived, students coordinated a school-wide election. In adherence to our state's laws regarding campaigning outside of polling places, they lined the sidewalks leading to the school's bus and drop off area, waving posters and chanting slogans for McCain or Obama. Mock voting booths were set up on the school stage, and classes came in at their scheduled times to vote. At the end of the day, when all of the votes were tallied, Obama edged out McCain by a slight margin. Several colorful write-in candidates made counting the vote entertaining. Our class served as the Electoral College for the school, and on the day that Obama was officially certified as the next president, we voted him in as well.

On Inauguration Day, we invited families to come and watch the swearing-in ceremony with us. We rarely know when we're actually living in a historical moment, and sharing an experience in which we all knew history was unfolding right in front of us was surreal. I remember looking around the packed classroom, listening to poet laureate Elizabeth Alexander as she spoke of "a praise song for walking forward in that light." I watched and listened in a room filled with multiple generations, overwhelmed with gratitude for these moments.

While the people of Washington, DC, were packing the streets for the presidential parade, we were marching through the neighborhood around the school with balloons, banners, and kazoos.

It culminated with a visit to a nearby childcare facility, where the workers loaded babies into wagons, toddlers perched atop adult shoulders, and preschoolers joined hands with twelve- and thirteen-year-olds as we marched around the school's parking lot and playground. We handed out balloons and flags and celebrated that we lived in a place where the people are allowed to participate in selecting the leaders of their people.

It's no surprise that the most popular event among the students was the one involving food. That year's presidential luncheon paid homage to Abraham Lincoln, but we decided to go with our own menu. We held a vote and eventually chose to have a feast that represented the entire nation, so students brought in dishes from all fifty states. We enjoyed peach cobbler from Georgia, salmon from Alaska, and potatoes from Idaho. It was a feast fit for a president!

In the years that have followed, I've often reflected on that day. Although our country was still feeling the fallout from 9/11 and there were conflicting feelings and opinions about the "global war on terror," my memories of the time are of a more unified America. In her poem, Alexander wrote about "love that casts a widening pool of light", a beautiful sentiment for the American people. As our country has become more divided over the years since that election, it makes me even more grateful to have been able to fully experience it with my students.

A few years ago, I found some pictures I'd taken during these months and shared them with some of the now-grown students. One of their responses blew my mind. When I taught Chelsea during her middle school years, her struggles would have challenged anyone, much less a girl who hadn't even made it into her teens yet. She had to make an extra effort in her classes because of a learning disability, and there were issues at home that often made concentrating on schoolwork difficult. When she saw the campaign pictures, she wrote to me, saying she remembered that day as "my first experience at campaigning, and I haven't stopped since." She'd graduated from Harvard with a degree that led her to Washington, DC, working on Capitol Hill in the office of Senator Elizabeth Warren. Today, she still lives in DC and works for an organization that endeavors to protect human rights and secure the future of the planet.

I Am

I am from plastic sleds
From Capri-Suns and Otter Pops
I am from the long, gravel driveway,
The site of generations of skinned knees
(rutted from rain, indented from the hooves of deer, goats and
horses)
I am from the giant maple
Tiny helicopters falling from the sky in spring, tricolored leaves
in autumn
I'm from hot chicken salad and generosity
From Emelene and Ira
I'm from hard work and make a difference
From "if you can't . . . then don't . . ." and "Bless your heart"
I'm from I surrender all and it is well with my soul
and a faith that became my why
I'm from Hope and Albuquerque
Fried okra y tacos
From Louis Rillos's move out of poverty through college and
football
And the frigid puddles that took Ira Yocom's nerves in WWII
Memories held in the walls of our home
In plastic sleeves of faded brown photo albums
And boxes of slides that can be viewed only in my mind
I am from this home, this land
Shovels full of dirt holding sweat from generations
Providing home

—Amanda, middle school principal

Chapter 9

To Teach and Protect?

I was teaching first grade on Tuesday, September 11, 2001, when my student teacher came running in to tell me that a plane had hit the World Trade Center and that it looked like it had been intentional. As the events of the day unfolded, I looked out over the faces of my students, skin tones ranging from pale peach to light tan to dark brown. Even though my own heart was aching, I knew they needed to know that they were safe. We went outside to the school courtyard and sat in a circle on the soft grass. As the sun shone down, in the midst of the horrors that were happening in our country, we told one another what we loved about each other. We listened to music and sang together; we shared our wishes for the world.

I'll always remember how fiercely I wanted to wrap them in my arms, shield them from the ugliness of those moments. Our school was located in an area where numerous petroleum companies had massive underground pipelines for transporting gas and oil. Fearing that they were vulnerable to attack, we began holding evacuation drills in the following weeks. Every few weeks, we'd have drills where we'd load the entire student body onto school buses as quickly as possible. The buses would then peel out of the school parking lot, headed to "safety". I had the same protective feelings that I experienced on 9/11 every time I shepherded my students to those buses. I just wanted them to know that I'd do everything

I could to keep them safe. My desire to protect my students drove me during those days of fear and uncertainty.

In April 1999, a friend and I left school to grab a bite to eat before a PTA meeting. At the restaurant, we watched in transfixed horror with all the other patrons as reports of a mass shooting at Columbine High School in Colorado began to unfold. Even though we were 1,500 miles away in Georgia, I grieved with that community. A little over a decade later, I found myself married to the social worker who'd been working at Columbine at the time of the shooting. We lived twenty minutes from the campus, and I started teaching in the district in 2011. Over the years, I worked alongside many who had experienced that day firsthand, either as students, teachers, families, or community members. A road I still travel on a daily basis is named after the teacher who was lost that day. I heard stories about teachers who huddled with students in classroom storage cabinets, refusing to come out for hours after the shooting. Injured students were transported to hospitals by teachers who would later become my friends. I've heard parents talk about waiting at a nearby park, watching as evacuated students crested the hill behind the school, scanning the crowd for the faces of their children. But the stories that stuck with me the most involve the way teachers tried to protect their students that day. And educators began to ask the unthinkable: could I lay down my life for my students?

After that tragedy, school safety drills soon included lockdown, lockout, and active shooter drills. I've seen children of all ages cry from stress and fear. My students would tell me about how they'd map out an escape plan in their head for each classroom they traveled to during the day so they wouldn't be caught off guard. No matter how many times I've experienced it, I've never gotten used to the sound of police imitating an intruder, beating on the classroom door during a drill, asking to be let in. At one point, we were encouraged to arm our students with anything available, and I have memories of seeing chair legs, protractors, scissors, and rulers gripped tightly in the hands of my huddled students as we silently waited for a drill to end.

During one memorable drill, we were instructed to allow the police officers to come into our classrooms so they could talk to everyone. When the officer came in, I was still on the floor with my students, back to the wall, out of sight of the windows. The officer told me that while we'd done a good job staying quiet and out of sight, the next time, I needed to stay by the door as the first line of defense. No college class or professional development can prepare you for such events. I will always resent that the one place of safety for many of our kids has the potential to become a battleground full of fear and trauma. When I hear controversy about the imagined harm a particular curriculum might cause our kids, I just shake my head. Somehow, I think the fear of being shot in the classroom trumps the potential harm that reading a book or hearing a history lecture can do.

We all know that the Columbine shooting was far from the last time a school would face such violence. Although I have no control over the actions that others choose to take, I've chosen to focus on the things I *can* control in my space. When people have asked me how I keep from being negatively affected by the stresses from outside the classroom that so often seep in and potentially damage the culture, I tell them my secret: close the door and teach. That may sound simplistic, but when I close that door, my focus centers on those within the room. And while I may not always be able to ensure their physical safety, it *is* in my control to do my best to create an environment of emotional safety.

I Am

I am creative and empathetic.
I wonder what the meaning of life is.
I hear secret songs as the wind blows past me.
I see dragons and fairies rising up through the glorious skies.
I want to be greeted by compassion and creativity wherever I go.
I am creative and empathetic.
I pretend that I am a leader, and slowly I become one.
I feel swirls of vibrant, magical emotions gliding through the air
around me.
I touch the fabric of reality.
I worry that I will leave this world without making an impact.
I cry when I listen to the broken stories and forgotten dreams of
my peers.
I am creative and empathetic.
I understand that people are stronger together than we are alone.
I say that there is hope for our future, because without hope we
are lost.
I dream about alternate realities and fantastical worlds.
I try to create my own reality and do what I love.
I hope that together we can work toward a better future.
I am creative and empathetic.

—Anja, age fifteen

Chapter 10

Hard Truths

Although the Supreme Court's decision in the Brown v. Board of Education case desegrated the nation's schools in 1954, for years my small Georgia town didn't see much change. I started first grade in 1966, and my first memory of having an African American classmate was during my second-grade year. By the time I started fifth grade, our community's "black school" was converted into a middle school for the entire district, and it was there that I became part of a more diverse student body for the first time. There was a lot of tension on both sides, and as I look back on it now, I realize we were a microcosm of society at the time. With Atlanta, the "Cradle of the Civil Rights Movement," only an hour or so away, it was impossible not to be aware of the historic events happening around the country, but it seemed as relevant as the news stories I'd periodically catch about the war in Vietnam. I remember overhearing my parents discuss Dr. King's assassination, but I felt like it was a world away from that little country town tucked into the red clay hills of Georgia.

Before long, the novelty of attending desegrated schools wore off, and the "new normal" became simply the "normal." Attitudes didn't change as quickly, though, and I was very aware of those in my world who weren't comfortable with how society was changing. Honestly, I never gave it much thought, and it would be many years before I began to realize that I had my own biases, many of which I was completely oblivious to. Once the process began, it seemed that I was confronting ugly truths about myself every time I turned around, and the chasm between reality and my own perceptions was vast.

During this time, I began to realize that teaching would change my perceptions of the world. As a young teacher in a school in inner-city Atlanta, I was definitely in the minority when it came to race. Given the mostly white community I grew up in, the feeling of being one of only a few was a new one, and I gained a new perspective as part of the minority. Several highly charged racial conflicts happened in our nation during my years there, and it was not always a comfortable place to teach. From the Rodney King case to O. J. Simpson's arrest and subsequent trial, along with less-publicized incidents, it was a time of racial tension in the country, and experiencing it in this environment was an education in and of itself. I was forced to confront my own blatant biases and blind spots, of which there were many. I learned so much from my teaching peers, but most of all, I learned from my students and their families.

I was still new to teaching and was working with a class of third graders in summer school. My '80s-permed hair was nothing special, but to my class of entirely African American children, it was a novelty. One humid summer afternoon, we were out at recess, and I was perched on a milk crate under an oak tree, surrounded by a group of five or six little girls. They were walking around me, discussing what types of styles they'd create if they had hair like mine. The conversation then moved from my hair to my jewelry, particularly my birthstone ring. They began to pepper me with questions about the type of stone, who gave it to me, and how old I'd be on my upcoming birthday.

The ring was on my left hand, which led to talk of wedding rings, and, of course, they eventually got around to asking if I was married. When I said that I wasn't, one of them nodded knowingly and said, "I've got a neighbor . . ." Then a puzzled look came over her face, and she asked, "Are you black or white?" When I told her

I was white, she said, "Oh, good, so is he." The memory of that hot Georgia afternoon still makes me smile. In the years since, I've encountered other young children who have a similar perception of race, and I always find it refreshing.

My friend was teaching kindergarten, and her blond hair and blue eyes were far different from the dark brown skin and black eyes of her students. A ruckus arose during center time one day, and she went over to investigate. A very indignant little boy pointed at a classmate and said, "He just said you were white!" His beloved teacher affirmed that she was, indeed, white, and he was in shock. When my friend reflected back, she told me it really made her reflect on the power of connection, the innocence of children, and most of all, it made her question how the world changes us as we get older.

Over the years, I've told these types of stories to friends, and the response has typically been, "Awwwww, see? Love sees no color! Wouldn't it be great if everyone could be like that?" How sweet. How refreshing. *How naïve.* Love may be blind, but it's not *color* blind. I've evolved to believe that love means "I see your color, and I value our differences."

One day, my high school students were working in small groups when a student loudly called another student a "cracker." The whole room froze, and in the silence, I marched over to the student who'd done the name-calling. Before I could make this a teachable moment, pontificating on appropriate language in Room 13, the other student quirked an eyebrow and said, "Actually, I prefer Saltine American." We all fell to laughing, and the situation was completely diffused with his humor, heading off a potentially volatile situation. While race relations are a very serious subject, it was nice to hear a response that not only took the tension out of the room but also brought us together in a shared moment of unbridled laughter. It did indeed become a teachable moment, but I wasn't the one who provided the learning.

The second year after I started teaching in the inner city school, a decades-long court case culminated with involuntary teacher transfers. In our district, there was a invisible line that divided the "white" and "black" parts of the community. Years before, a group of black parents had filed a lawsuit against the district which alleged that there were discrepancies in the education that students were receiving on each end of the county, with more quality instruction and money going towards the area where mostly white students attended. In his ruling, the judge found that curriculum and funding differences were only part of the inequities. A large percentage of more experienced, white teachers worked in the area of the district where most of the students were white. In the other area, there tended to be less experienced teachers, and they were part of the racial majority. As part of his decision, the judge mandated that white, more experienced teachers be transferred via lottery to the other end of the county. It was a time of upheaval for veteran teachers, some of whom had been in the same school their whole career. As a relatively inexperienced teacher at the end of the county that was receiving transfers, I was given the choice of remaining in my school or transferring, and I chose to stay where I was. I never expected the resentment that some of the educators who'd been transferred would feel towards me for actually *choosing* to stay in a school where they had been forcefully placed. I learned so much from that experience. The negativity that came with several of the transferees made me determined to never allow myself to become so bitter in my career, regardless of circumstances. That lesson has stayed with me. Some of those teachers caused extreme emotional turmoil in their students. But the greater lesson for me was realizing how much I had to learn and grow in my understanding of race relations. I'm still learning.

One year, I helped chaperone a group of middle school students on a trip to the Florida Keys. We swam with the dolphins, wrote with squid ink, listened to the croak of alligators in the swamps, rode on airboats through the Everglades, and kayaked in the mangroves. It was truly a trip to remember, but one incident almost overshadowed everything else for me. We'd all been looking forward to scuba diving in the coral reef off Marathon Key. Our group consisted of an almost even mix of white and African American kids, and although it hadn't seemed to be an issue for anyone so far, it obviously was for the worker who was handing out wet suits.

He was a burly, middle-aged white man, face covered with a scraggly beard and dominated by a large red nose that had prominent veins running through it. I stood in line, took my wet suit, and was headed off to put it on when I noticed an African American colleague standing off to the side watching the process, holding her wet suit, making no move to put it on. I could tell by the look on her face that she was disturbed about something, so I went to check on her. Wordlessly, she held out her wet suit, and while my own suit was pristine, with no patches or poorly concealed holes, hers had more repaired areas than not. At first, I just thought the supplies were running low, and as a result, he'd resorted to giving out used, faded, patched wet suits, but there were many completely intact suits still hanging up, ready for divers. I began to look at the suits that had been given out to our students, and without exception, the white kids had suits in the same perfect condition as mine, and every African American student had a suit in the same condition as my colleague's. Every. Single. One.

At first, I was speechless, and then I got mad. I went to the proprietor, showing him my suit and then the one my friend had been given. I'd like to say I politely requested that we all be given suits in the same condition as my own, but it was actually more of a demand. I didn't confront him on the subtle way he'd shown his prejudice, and we all headed to the water in shiny suits without patches. I've always wished I'd been more vocal about how wrong it was.

Growing up in a primarily white community in the deep South, I was aware of racial tensions from a young age. And living and working in a community in which I was in the minority meant that I was constantly learning and having to confront my own blind spots. I can change my hair color, I can lose weight—heck, I can even go to a tanning bed to alter my skin tone. But at the end of the day, I can't change the skin I was born into. I can only hope to be more aware, open, and sensitive. Perhaps acknowledging our differences is the most loving thing we can do for one another.

I Am

I am funny and a daredevil.
I wonder why we can't send everyone to space
I hear Burn, the dragon, whispering her evil plan to
become queen
I see fiery colored Sky Wings
I want to have a pet Sky Wing dragon
I am funny and a daredevil.

I pretend to like my sister's drawings, but sometimes I don't
I feel blistering hot heat in my brain
I touch hard dragon scales that feel like guitar picks
I worry that my friends will stop being my friend
I cry and get angry when people pick on my sister
I am funny and a daredevil.

I understand that dinosaurs existed
I say Bigfoot is real
I dream about having an Ender 3D printer
I try hard on my reading and writing
I hope for a green Jeep Wrangler
I am funny and a daredevil.

—Zach, age ten

Chapter 11

LIPS and SNIPS

Any teacher who's taught for any amount of time has had at least one of THOSE years when a career change feels inevitable. In those times, the thought of being an orangutan pee collector, a sewer cleaner, or even the person who cleans up amusement park vomit can be more appealing than one more day in the classroom. One of those years occurred for me when I was teaching a group of seventh graders who made every day a challenge, to say the least. It was impossible to get through a lesson without some type of interruption every, oh, twenty seconds or so. It was like a living version of Whack-a-Mole every single day, and all of my best tried-and-true behavioral management plans proved futile. To make matters worse, I injured my back that year and was in excruciating pain for weeks on end. During the school day, I didn't dare take the hydrocodone I'd been prescribed—this crew was unmanageable *without* being impaired—but ibuprofen didn't put a dent in the chaos those seventh graders wrought on a daily basis. I'm still convinced that there was a major disruption in the cosmos during the period of time when those children were conceived.

Finally, after a particularly horrible day of back pain and hormone-driven tweenage angst, I sat down on my Aylio coccyx orthopedic foam seat cushion, popped a couple of Tylenol, and wondered how I was going to survive the rest of the school year. After crossing shock collars, waterboarding, and duct tape off the list, I grabbed a handful of index cards and a tube of burgundy lipstick. I applied the lipstick and promptly kissed sixty cards. I laminated them, and the next day, I presented my newest attempt at winning Survivor Seventh Grade: Learning Interruption Passes (LIPS). Each student was given two LIPS at the start of class, and whenever an interruption occurred through the fifty-minute period, they had to surrender a card. After a few days in which students tried to bargain with one another for extra LIPS, life improved, at least to the extent that I canceled my plans to start a Teachers Anonymous chapter and rescinded my application for Walmart greeter. My back pain didn't subside, but I felt good about the progress I was making in actually getting through lessons. I had won the battle, if not the war.

Then one day after class, Leo asked if he could talk to me. Now, Leo was my bright spot in a sea of darkness that year. He was kind to everyone, had a luminous smile that was almost always present, and had pretty much been the human equivalent of Valium for me, even before my back went out. After the last student had left the room, I beckoned for Leo to join me at my desk. I was getting pretty pumped about the praise that was about to be heaped on me for my transformative new LIPS discipline program. Instead, Leo laid out three index cards in front of me, each of which had a picture of a pair of scissors glued onto the front. Without giving me the opportunity to speak, he haltingly began to explain his idea. It seemed that the pain generated by my back injury had begun to warp my personality. According to Leo, I had become extremely "snippy," and he missed the teacher I'd been prior to getting hurt. He explained that he would like permission to hold up a SNIP card whenever the possessed version of his teacher came out, with the hope that three per class period would be enough.

I was gobsmacked, yet I knew that this blond-headed ray of sunshine was spot on. Somehow, I had morphed into someone I hardly recognized. Back pain and a challenging class notwithstanding, I had evolved into a negative version of myself that I didn't even know existed. Thanking Leo for caring enough to help me change *my* behavior, I told him that we'd start using SNIPS the next day. I told the entire class about Leo's idea, and I apologized for allowing the situation with my back pain to derail me from being the teacher they deserved.

I'd like to say that the behavior of the class magically changed and that I got well so quickly, I was soon cartwheeling into school each day henceforth, but the truth is that the challenges remained. What *did* change, though, was my attitude. Leo had reminded me that he and his peers deserved the best I had to give. I was unable to speed up the healing process for my back or perform lobotomies for those with the most obnoxious behaviors, but I *could* change how I responded to the challenges. And I did. (But I also counted down every minute of what seemed like the 649 days left in that school year!)

This was when I began to think a lot about what I began to call "Their Time." Although I'd always tried to be fully present each day with my students, this experience made me even more aware that while teaching will provide many years for me to get it right, my students have just this short window of time. In spite of the heroics that teachers perform every day, we are ultimately only human. We will hit rough patches, times in which we're not at our best. But I've always tried to remember that even though I get a redo every year, my students don't get that same re-start. They'll only be this age once, and this is our one opportunity to do right by them. This is THEIR time.

Teaching Tidbit Lesson 4:
The Comedy Writes Itself

When a parent brings in a VHS cassette on which he's taped over a movie in order to record something for your class, preview it ahead of time. You may find that while the program is indeed geared to your current curriculum, there could be some glitches with the technology. And you may have to throw your body over the TV screen in order to spare your fourth graders further viewing of the hard-core porn video that has just interrupted a Dr. Martin Luther King Jr. biography. Your "I Have a Dream Moment" quickly morphs into a nightmare.

When disposable cameras come out, students will be completely enthralled with them. When you chaperone fourth graders on an overnight field trip, one of them may be taking pictures with three disposable cameras that he talks about incessantly. When you return home and ask that student where his cameras are, he may tell you that he threw them out. After all, they were disposable, and the pictures were going to magically appear in the film-processing kiosk near his house.

When you send home a note about two of your kindergarten students stabbing one another with holly leaves, their parents may come to school very upset that you're being sacrilegious. Because why would you even have something holy in an elementary school? Such leaves should be left in church.

If you want to prank one of your most rambunctious seventh-grade boys on April Fools' Day by setting up a meeting with your principal in which the student is told, "We know what you did . . .," be prepared. Said student may start confessing to so many things that you will have to interrupt the litany before he is suspended.

You may be in on an interview someday when the prospective teacher says that she's very tech savvy, utilizing the overhead "protector" almost daily.

She doesn't get the job.

If you're busily getting materials together for your next lesson and call out to your middle school class to please "flip off" the projector, be prepared for what happens next.

A student may think it's appropriate to come to class wearing only a cardboard box around his privates because it's his eighteenth birthday and he's now a legal adult and can do whatever he wants.

When teaching remotely during a pandemic, you don't expect to see a parent walking behind his child in his boxers. Bright green ones. That aren't clean.

As well, during pandemic teaching, a student may remember to turn off their device's camera but not the sound when they use the bathroom.

In yet another interview, an applicant may submit her resume with her name and address in the proper places. She may also leave all of the Latin that was on the template, so the rest of the resume reads, "Lorem ipsum dolor . . ."

She doesn't get the job either.

Someday a 14 year-old may tell you that she wants to blow up the sun, and when you ask her what she'd put in its place, she may immediately reply, "A giant picture of Rick Astley".

Chapter 12

A Land of Immigrants

When we had returned to in-person learning after the Covid pandemic, I attended a meeting with fellow educators about our caseload for the coming school year. One of our upcoming freshmen was the child of undocumented parents and, by all accounts, was an incredibly bright, high-achieving student. In the course of our conversation, I learned that his family was evicted at the beginning of the Covid lockdown. Their status kept them from appealing the eviction—they were afraid to draw attention to themselves. Because they weren't documented, they weren't eligible for any assistance. At one of the most stressful, potentially deadly periods in our country's history, this student and his family were thrust into a world of uncertainty and danger. Welcome to the American Dream.

I believe in legal immigration. I believe we need sensible legislation for those who wish to move to the US. But more than that, I believe in the dignity of human beings, and I absolutely do NOT believe that people are illegal. Nor are they "aliens." And I will never, ever be okay with children being criminalized because their parents had the audacity to want a better life for their family.

Over the course of ten years, I taught three sisters, all of whom were honor students throughout their school careers. Their father worked twelve hours a day, six days a week in a restaurant, while their mother cleaned houses in spite of debilitating health issues.

While the girls were all born in the US, these hard-working parents were undocumented. All three girls were bright, optimistic, and funny, so when the youngest, Lily, became withdrawn during her freshman year, I reached out to see if I could help. Through sobs, she told me she didn't want to be in school and that she'd been begging her parents to let her stay home all week. There had been stories in the news that month about undocumented workers being arrested in raids at their places of employment. She was terrified that she was going to go home one afternoon and find that her parents had been detained. In her youthful innocence, she thought that if she could go to work with them, her mere presence would stop it from happening.

Leisa, her older sister, once gave a class presentation about why she loves Christmas. As carols softly played over Spotify, she took us into her world of decorating their small apartment with lights and tinsel; even the bird cage was decorated. On Christmas Eve, her parents would sit their three girls side-by-side on a couch and proceed to tell them why they are *their* version of the American Dream. She said that they say the same thing every year, and everyone gets emotional, in spite of the fact that it's the same words each time. The oldest daughter, Jenna, is almost through with nursing school, having worked her own way through college. It's hard to believe that there are those who want to criminalize these parents, who work day in and day out to raise their daughters to be good people who make a difference in the world. In fact, I've taught children of US citizens who weren't raised with nearly the same attention and care.

I was teaching a unit on immigration to a seventh-grade social studies class. During one lesson, Norberto suddenly put his head on his desk, shoulders shaking with sobs. The room grew quiet as everyone gave him some space. He finally told us about the flashback he was having as we talked about people immigrating to the US. In his mind, he was riding on his father's shoulders as they waded across the Rio Grande. The waters rose higher and higher as he watched, until they were just below his father's chin. Frightened, he cried and pleaded with his parents to turn around. Both told him they had to keep going, that this was a risk they were willing to take because they wanted him to have a better life than they could provide for him in Mexico.

I have a hard time understanding why it is criminal to want to provide for your family. It's easy to rail about illegal immigration—the cost, the impact on healthcare and education—but behind the political talking points, these are human beings. Some are fleeing for their lives, others hope for a quality education, but all want better lives than the ones they left behind. I can't change the system, but there is one thing I can and will do. As long as I am teaching, I will proudly give their children my very best so that the sacrifices of their parents are not in vain.

I Am

I am an artist and kind.
I wonder how to make a toy that you can play with forever
I hear a unicorn eating pizza
I see big pink unicorns
I want my mom and dad to not die
I am an artist and kind.

I pretend to like tomatoes but I don't
I feel bunnies hugging me
I touch a chocolate ocean
I worry that my brother has a pocket knife
I cry when I look at puppies that might die
I am an artist and kind.

I understand that dogs are really cute
I say mermaids are real
I dream about being an artist and teaching others to do art
I try to climb up my bed without the ladder
I hope that somebody in the world will clean up all the trash in
the ocean
I am an artist and kind.

—Elena, age seven

Chapter 13

Love in Any Language

Have you ever taken an impulsive jump into a situation and realized too late that you were in over your head? Yeah, well, me too, more times than I'll admit to, and a prime example is the year I decided to go work in a school simply because I loved the principal. Having worked as a teacher in a school where he was an assistant principal, I would have followed him anywhere. I eagerly agreed to a second-grade position, and given the fact that internet access involved a dial-up connection, and even that wasn't commonplace, I went in without knowing anything about the school.

Confident in my ability to teach *any*one, *any*time, *any*where, I found that belief put to the test the first day I greeted my new class—their shining faces watching me with eager anticipation just like any other year. But this time, my class was composed of *all* non-English speakers. The room reverberated with the sounds of voices speaking Farsi, Spanish, Bosnian, Nepalese, Arabic, Burmese, Hindi, Khmer, Vietnamese, Korean, Russian, and more. The community is still home to one of the highest concentrations of foreign-born citizens in the country. Teaching there was like experiencing a miniature United Nations gathering every day, and I was completely flummoxed as to how to bring this diverse group of beautiful children together as a unit—a family. But I buckled up, enrolled in an English as a Second Language program, and let the children teach *me* how to teach them.

Those with a rudimentary grasp of English would volunteer to translate for their peers. I developed my own version of sign language during read-alouds, becoming a contortionist for some lessons. We labeled *everything*, and I had the students label things for me in their native languages. I tried to make every lesson hands-on as much as possible. Great conversations developed around Crabby and Gabby, our cockatiels; Rainbow, our sun conure; and Bailey Bunny. And it didn't take long before I realized I was dealing with some of the most intelligent children I'd ever met. They were spilling over with talents and gifts that would fly under the radar, limiting their access to advanced curriculum, because the current system of testing was biased toward native English speakers. As they learned to speak English, I was astounded by how quickly they picked it up, and their ability to switch back and forth from English to their native language blew my mind. Nearly every student was a refugee, and they came with life experiences that would crush most adults.

One family's story is still painful to think about. Karina, at age six, was living on the streets of Mexico with her two younger brothers. They were basically "street urchins," begging for food, living in the trees outside their village. It was months before anyone realized the children had been abandoned by their single mother. Once it came to light, they were sent to live in the US with their aunt. Yet they, and all of the children, somehow retained such zest and love for life. They appreciated the littlest things, opening my eyes to how much I took for granted.

When a new student spoke his or her first unprompted words of English, we celebrated! I'd call the whole class over, tell them the words that had been spoken, and we'd dance and jump around like a bunch of *gente loca*. And then Luis arrived from El Salvador. Luis did *not* want to speak anything except his native tongue. We cajoled, teased, and practically demanded that he try, but it didn't matter; he was not going to budge. After almost a month of this, we were outside on the playground one day when Luis rushed up to me and breathlessly exclaimed, "Miss Lee! Abaz say, '*^%@ you!'" I stood there, dumbfounded. LUIS SPOKE ENGLISH! We needed to celebrate! But—I don't think I've ever been so conflicted in my professional life before or since! I finally gathered everyone together and told them that we needed to celebrate because Luis had spoken English for the first time. When Karina inquired as to what he'd said, I stumbled around for the right words and finally settled on, "Well, he said a curse word." In unison, they all began chanting, "He said a curse word! He said a curse word!" And I joined in with the chanting, as we all relished the moment.

At parent-teacher conferences that November, I met with a dad who was raising two sons and a daughter by himself. In broken English, he proudly told me about the basketball, boxing gloves, and art set he'd put on layaway for Christmas. I mentioned this to one of my neighbors, and before I knew it, the community had all come together to give each student and family in my class a special holiday. The mayor dressed as Santa, and when he got to school on the day of the celebration, he got on the intercom and gave a hearty HO! HO! HO! I will never forget the looks on those faces—white, brown, black—staring up at the loudspeaker as they jumped up and down screaming, "Santa!"—a name that needed no translation. The room was packed with my neighbors and the families of the students, as well as a local news station who did a story on the event. I was so struck by the love and connection between a group of people who, for the most part, couldn't speak to one another in a common language.

When Earth Day rolled around, I was in a meeting with other teachers to work on lesson plans for that week. We were discussing charts to fill in, essay ideas, and art projects involving flowers when I suddenly decided that my class was going to build a pond in the enclosed courtyard across from our classroom. Every student lived in an apartment, and they didn't get much time to play outside.

When they did, it was in small, cramped playgrounds or the small patches of grass in front of their apartments.

The day after I decided on the Great Pond Adventure, I came to school with as many shovels as I could borrow, and the kids and I started to dig. And dig. By the end of the week, we were all sporting blisters on our hands, but there was a hole in the ground ready for us to fill. The pond liner went in, a pump was installed, and we collected rocks from around the neighborhood. We transplanted numerous plants between the rocks; eggs hatched into ducks that, as soon as they were able, were swimming in our pond. We added some colorful koi, a few tadpoles that grew into croaking frogs, and even a few chubby crawdads. Students were disappointed when the project ended, so we moved a little farther down the courtyard and built a butterfly garden. We hatched painted lady butterflies from caterpillars and had ceremonies in which we watched them fly for the first time. We may not have covered all of the science objectives for second grade that year, but what the students *did* learn far surpassed anything they'd have read in a textbook or worksheet packet.

The end of the year arrived long before I was ready, and I was heartbroken about saying goodbye to my sweet kids, so I decided to move up to the next grade with them. As you can imagine, third grade with this group brought many more experiences and memories. One of my all-time favorite teaching experiences happened that fall when we were studying the Creek and Cherokee tribes. We turned our classroom into a Native village, and for two weeks, everything we did in class was accomplished from inside teepees and longhouses. Math and science lessons involved pounding corn into cornmeal, measuring it out, and making fried bread. We studied legends and myths and wrote our own for each culture. One day, as I was talking about how central the campfire was to the tribes, I made an offhand comment about how everyone understands how special it feels to sit around a roaring campfire. Judging from the clueless looks on their faces, I realized that none of these apartment-dwelling children had ever experienced sitting around a campfire. We marched through the neighborhood, scouring the ground for rocks, sticks, and logs. Once back at the school, we made a beautiful fire in the enclosed courtyard right next to our classroom. As we sat there, I watched the magic happen. Those children gazed into the flames, completely transfixed. We read stories and poetry as the fire crackled and popped. I couldn't have scripted a better moment. And then we heard the sirens. You see, since the courtyard was in the middle of the school, it looked from a distance like the school was on fire. The next thing I knew, every administrator in the building was standing at the windows overlooking the courtyard. I'm not quite sure what they saw, but judging by the looks on their faces, it wasn't magic. The main thing I remember is reading my principal's lips as he repeated over and over, "What. Are. You. Doing?" and seeing one of the assistant principals shaking her head and wagging one pointer finger back and forth. Once the dust (ashes?) settled, I had time to reflect on the experience. I determined that given the chance, I'd do it all over again just to see those precious faces aglow with the light of the flames, caught up in the magic.

Emory University was not far from our campus, and one of the professors sponsored an annual event for the patients at Emory's Children's Hospital. He approached me with the idea of making some type of toy that the hospitalized children could enjoy. The only requirement, besides being safe to play with, was that it had to be made completely out of recycled materials. After discussing and debating a number of ideas, the class finally decided to build a dollhouse. Students came to school loaded with scraps of fabric, leftover tile and carpet, paper towel rolls—anything that looked like it could be repurposed for a new life in our dollhouse. They created tables from empty thread spools, lamps were fashioned from door stops, and furniture was finely crafted from sticks and rocks that we found lying around outside the school. CNN came out to record when, with great ceremony, the professor brought a group of his graduate students to the school to pick the house up. Word soon got back to us that it was being moved from department to department in the hospital, not just the children's section, because it was such a hit. In retrospect, it greatly resembled the Weasley home, the Burrow, in the Harry Potter series. But the pride that those kids took in their tilted, eclectic cardboard creation was indescribable.

That fall, *Harry Potter and the Sorcerer's Stone,* the first book in J. K. Rowling's series, was rapidly becoming a global phenomenon, so I decided to develop curriculum that met district standards while using Hogwarts and its inhabitants as the inspiration. Remember the magic I knew was going to unfold with these third graders? Well, the reality was so much greater than my expectations. Rowling's magical world transcended language, and Harry, Hermione, Ron, Hagrid, and Dumbledore became a part of our daily lives. My student's reading scores soared that year, and I credit it to Hogwarts and its inhabitants. In fact, Maria, the student whose father inspired the Great Christmas Celebration of the previous year, had some of the highest scores in the district.

The next year, the first *Harry Potter* movie came out, and those wonderful kids had moved on to fourth grade while I was now teaching first. Although I was no longer their teacher, we decided to form a Harry Potter Club that met several times a week during lunch to continue reading the series. We were all so incredibly excited about the movie. I went to every thrift store in the area and bought up all the graduation robes I could find. We stitched together hats and made wands, and the local news came out to do a story on our club. As a result of the publicity, we were showered with more Harry Potter merch than I knew existed, as well as tickets for the movie premiere. We all showed up at the theater to watch it together. My life could have ended right then and there, and I'd have been completely happy.

Over my time working in this school, I became more and more convinced that these students had intelligence and potential like none I'd ever seen, which led me to pursue a degree in gifted and talented education, and to this day, I advocate for appropriate testing and higher level instruction for diverse learners. They have so much to give and to teach all of us.

I Am

I am skilled but troubled
I wonder why people are the way they are
I hear the voice of a passing ghost
I see entire worlds in front of me
I want to redefine myself as worthy
I am skilled but troubled.

I pretend to have nothing to hide
I feel my inescapable imagination
I touch the chains linking the world's past and mine
I worry that I'll never change for better
I cry because sometimes I change for worse
I am skilled but troubled.

I understand imperfection is inevitable, if not beneficial
I say why worship evil when there's so much good
I dream of going overseas with no fear of humiliation
I try to escape my demons
I hope I will turn out okay
I am skilled but troubled.

—Anonymous

Chapter 14

You Just Gotta Laugh

One year, I convinced my middle school principal to let me ditch traditional desks and chairs and replace them with couches, recliners, ottomans, and lap desks. Combined with the lamps I used instead of overhead lighting, it made for a cozy space to live, learn, and laugh. I had a comfortable stool on which I perched at the front of the room as we engaged in memorable discussions about the Trail of Tears, political parties, and global warming. The memories of those days remain some of the best of my career.

It is important that you know that during those years, I went through a phase in which I did most of my teaching in a skirt. (Thank goodness, some fads fade.) *And* it never occurred to me that my students were eye level with the area just below my waist. Oh, and I tend to move a lot when I teach. One day, after my eighth graders had filed out of the room, I noticed a folded piece of paper left behind on one of the couches. It looked suspiciously like a note, and I hurried over to get caught up on the latest bit of drama that was circulating among my students. To my consternation, the note was not about the teens who traveled in and out of my room every day. It was a brief note about *me*: "You can see up her skirt. Again." Unbeknownst to me, I'd been exposing my unmentionables to twelve- and thirteen-year-old children on a daily basis. But even worse, it had apparently become a source of gossip—I'd become THAT teacher. (For me, it had been one of my middle school math teachers. She was tall, thin, very pale, with dark hair carefully teased into a beehive, and she wore brilliantly bright red lipstick. I surreptitiously watched every day for her to pull out her compact and pluck her nose hairs when we were supposed to be working independently. Maybe that's why I've never liked math, but I digress.)

It wasn't hard to recognize the swirly handwriting, with hearts for dots on the i's, as that of one of my favorite students, Edwina. My first reaction was to go find her, deliver a stern lecture about writing notes in class—*especially notes that made fun of ME*–and assign a punishment. Since this was a social studies class, I thought some of the methods employed by the ancient Romans might be appropriate, but I lacked a rack or heretic's fork, so I knew I had to be creative. What could I do to make a lasting impression?

The next day, I intentionally wore a skirt. *Again.* (See what I did there?) When Edwina's class arrived, I went through my usual greeting, took roll, handed out a quiz, and then perched myself atop my throne. And I waited. It didn't take long. When Edwina looked up from her paper to gaze around the room, I tried to catch her eye. It took a few times before she took the bait and looked. And it was GLORIOUS. I casually lifted my skirt so she could see what was underneath and, before anyone else noticed, put it back in place. Now that sounds really creepy, so let me explain. I not only had on a pair of shorts under the skirt, but I had pinned a sign underneath as well. It read, "Edwina, stop writing notes in class." Her face took on a hue that I've never seen before or since. I, on the other hand, acted as if nothing was amiss. I continued to survey my kingdom, always on the lookout for another chance to flash my . . . ahmmmm, sign. Not a word was spoken. At the end of class, Edwina ran up to me and just said, "I promise" and threw her arms around me.

We both learned a lesson as a result of this experience. I was able to prevent a lifetime of future therapy (for them, not me) by keeping my knees closed and skirt down. And Edwina—well, I hope that her life lesson was NOT that I liked purple undies. I hope she realized that humor can make the most awkward situations a learning experience.

The best teachers I've known have had the ability to not take themselves too seriously. They laugh a lot. Although I've always been as serious as can be about my job, it's hard to think of a day when I didn't laugh with my students. Often, that humor comes at my expense, but I guess it's a lesson in and of itself to see an adult who's not afraid to laugh at herself.

I love teaching history, and the Civil War is one of my favorite topics. Growing up in Georgia, I was raised with stories of the War of Northern Aggression as Sherman marched south to Savannah. It is hard to drive more than a mile in Georgia without seeing a marker commemorating some type of historical event that happened during those years. I took students to Andersonville, the infamous Confederate prisoner of war camp, where row after row of white gravestones give silent testimony to the brutalities of a war that pitted brother against brother. When I began teaching social studies in Colorado, I realized my eighth graders had little knowledge of that era. It was up to me to bring it to life, and I was in my element. I shared the tales that had been told by my Uncle Judge about the Yamn Dankees, stories that had been passed down from one generation to the next, about when Sherman's army made camp for weeks in my kinfolk's pastures. I knew a ghost story about every region we studied, and we'd turn out the lights, close the blinds, and get spooked together with only a candle for light.

Finally, the day I had been waiting for arrived. I began leading them through the 1864 Battle of Atlanta. It wasn't hard to imagine that we smelled the acrid smoke as the fires burned all around us. Wagons being flung about by panicked teams of horses as they careened through the streets, people fleeing the carnage dodged in and out of their paths. Shells from Sherman's army bombarded the city, and the screams of animals and humans mingled with the smell of scorched earth. I stopped and looked out over my rapt (captive?)

audience, breathing hard from the exertion of running for my life among the flames. Not one of the eighth graders moved. They were silent, waiting to hear what was coming next. I had them in the palm of my hand. As I surveyed my domain, I knew that I had been created for this moment. No teacher *in the history of teachering* had ever painted such a realistic, all-encompassing picture. It was my moment, and I reveled in it.

Then Colton raised his hand. I took a deep breath, rearranged my disheveled clothing that had been rendered askew in the battle, and prepared myself to receive his effusive compliments. I waited for his tears to fall as he told me how he'd never forget this moment. How it had changed his life. I imagined he was about to tell me that in the last half hour, he had changed his future plans from professional baseball player to history teacher. I paused, gazing around to ensure that everyone witnessed the moment.

In the silence of the battlefield, I said, "Yes, Colton."

"Ms. Lee, were you scared?"

There was utter silence. No one laughed. They were all waiting for my response. I stood with my mouth agape, chagrined that my Emmy award for Most Inspiring Performance by a Teacher was slipping through my fingers. Finally, I dissolved into a fit of laughter, one of those where the more you try to get control, the more you lose it. In retrospect, I'd like to think that my inspired teaching was so mesmerizing that it was easily mistaken for a firsthand account. And as memorable as my vivid lecture may have been, seeing me running across the hall to the bathroom with my legs crossed made an equally unforgettable impression.

Experiencing humorous moments together is a sure way to bring us closer to those we teach. But we can't have a relationship with students who don't show up for school, obviously. I've been known to take matters into my own hands when it comes to getting my kids into the building. I could tell you numerous stories of driving by various homes on my way to school to rouse kids and bring them with me to school. But my favorite by far is the story of my lovable, goofy Hector.

I was teaching middle school at the time, and Hector was in my first-period humanities class. *IF* he came to school, he was always late, and I could go weeks at a time without seeing him at all, even though he often made it in later in the day, long after the first bell had rung. Toward the end of our first semester together, I discovered Hector lived in an apartment building just a few blocks from the school. That was all I needed. The very next day, I rounded up the entire class, and we headed to Hector's complex to wake him up and bring him to school with us.

Well, it turned out his apartment was on the second floor, and we didn't have a way into the building. One of his friends knew where Hector's bedroom was located, though, and the class eagerly began gathering stones to fling at his window. I managed to talk them off the ledge, and I located a wet string mop hanging on a balcony. Before I thought it through completely, I had grabbed the mop and was banging on his window. Truly the highlight of the semester for all of us!

I wish I could say that this magically cured Hector's attendance issues, but it didn't. However, we did see him several times a week after that, which was a huge improvement. And he never, ever forgot that he had a teacher crazy enough to come bang on his window with a mop to get him to school! (I would imagine no one else in the class ever forgot it either.)

At one point in my career, I was able to teach the same students in both middle and high school, and Beth was one of them. I was very aware of the trauma she carried with her. It typically emerged as volatile bursts of anger, so when she came down to my room freshman year screaming about wanting to cause bodily harm to her math teacher, I knew she needed to vent. I also knew that Beth's typical manner of letting off steam could get her suspended from school, so I pulled her into the teacher's kitchen, located right off the classroom. Since it wasn't lunch, we had the room to ourselves, which turned out to be a good thing.

This time Beth's venting had a different feel from any other time I'd seen her allow her anger to take control. For the first time in the three years I'd known her, she said, "I just want to break something, then I'd feel better!" Knowing that it usually took hours to calm her, I was willing to give it a try. I looked around the kitchen and saw a white ceramic plate that was on top of the microwave. I handed it to her and said, "Break it!" She looked at me incredulously and said, "For real?" When I nodded, she held the plate high over her head and then slammed it down onto the floor so hard that it left a noticeable dent. She looked up at me and said, "Wow. I. Feel. Better." I knew we needed to talk about the feelings behind what had happened, so as we picked up pieces of the plate, I began probing. As we cleaned and talked, so many other feelings came out rather than just the intense anger she'd come in with. For the rest of high school, Beth would bring up that day, and we took more than one excursion into the kitchen to laugh over the dent in the tile. I never did find out who the plate belonged to.

Not long after that, I went to the dollar store and stocked up on white ceramic plates. If a student was struggling in a way that I knew would likely lead to a violent outburst, I'd hand them a plate and a Sharpie. I'd tell them to write whatever they wanted on the plate about how they were feeling. Once they did, we would go outside to a large rock near the school's parking lot. There, they'd smash the plate, and if it didn't break into small enough pieces, they'd pick it up and do it again. And again. Sometimes, they screamed out as they broke the plate, but not always. And I found that more often than not, students asked to clean up the pieces themselves, without any assistance from me. It seemed to be part of the whole experience—the smashing and breaking and then literally picking up the pieces. Never once did a student leave even one shard of plate behind.

I began to call these experiences "Things to get off our plate." Over the years, not one student got into trouble afterward, at least not because of the situation that brought them there in the first place. The whole experience of getting their feelings out physically and emotionally and then cleaning up afterward helped them resume their day without any more drama. I know that there is some controversy about using physical actions to help with anger management. Personally, I think that writing the words on the plate, smashing it, then talking about it while we cleaned up was more than just a physical release. And each time, I'd get feedback about how much better they felt once we headed back inside.

The dent in the tile is still there.

Teaching Tidbit Lesson 5:
Don't Take Yourself So Seriously

If you answer the phone in the main office as a favor to the secretaries who are otherwise occupied with beginning-of-the-year chaos, be prepared for questions about what families need to bring in order to register their students. And make sure your answer doesn't combine proof of residence and birth certificate, thus uttering the phrase, "Make sure you bring proof of birth control."

If you know you don't see things in the same manner as, say, an architect or interior designer, it might be good to have someone check your attempts at decorating your classroom. Otherwise, at the end of the year, your student teacher may ask you, "I've always wondered. How come you prefer to have everything hanging crooked on the walls?" You might have never even noticed.

If you sleepily grab a pair of pants out of the hamper because you slept through the alarm and didn't have time to iron, ensure that the pant leg isn't hiding a pair of rumpled underpants. If you do, you might find yourself walking down the hallway with your fourth graders when the bloomers fall to the ground, having worked their way down your pant leg. Even a class full of kids who rarely pay attention to you will choose this moment to change that behavior.

If you accidentally wear a pair of mismatched shoes and think no one will notice, you're almost right. The adults won't.

You may get a Christmas present you really love from a student, only to learn it was shoplifted. You may be really conflicted.

Chapter 15

Everyone Can Give

The Dalai Lama wrote, "No one is so poor that they cannot enrich the lives of others with kindness and compassion, as these come from the heart, not your purse." The majority of my career has been spent in schools that were not located in affluent zip codes. Although most of the families with whom I've worked were not materially blessed, it has always been important to me to give my students opportunities to serve and give to others. Some of these opportunities were more involved than others, but I believe that all my students found value in each experience.

My elementary and middle school students were enthusiastic supporters of the American Cancer Society's Relay for Life. I'll always remember watching my crew in their tie-dyed purple and white shirts, holding signs that proclaimed each of them to be a "One-Eyed, One-Horned Flying Purple Cancer Beater." We participated in that for several years, and spending the night in a stadium packed with young people was exhausting and amazing. We raised money for cancer research, and when all 400 of us gathered for the lighting of the luminaries to honor those whose lives have been affected by the disease, the wonder far outweighed the exhaustion.

When a new chai tea establishment was in the process of renovating a building across from our middle school, my students decided to do something to welcome them to the community. For a month, we spent several afternoons each week across the street, weeding, planting flowers, and picking up trash. A group of the more enterprising kids found uses for the yards and yards of vines we pulled up. If you ever find yourself in need of a jump rope and don't have one handy, I've seen firsthand how well vines can work! When the shop opened, the owner hired several of my students to sweep the porches before school each morning, and after school, we'd often take musical instruments over for a jam session. Our work to help the shop open up gave all of us a sense of ownership and pride.

I was teaching seventh and eighth graders in a Title I middle school, and the ninth anniversary of 9/11 was a couple of weeks away. We were located right next to a fire station, so we decided to spearhead a school-wide drive to take cards, meals, and gifts to the firefighters to thank them for their service to our community, and to honor their fallen NYC brothers and sisters. Thanks to the generosity of our school community, we fed the entire station for a week. They papered the walls of their firehouse with notes from our students, families, and teachers. We got to ride up in the bucket of one of the engines. Watching the interactions between those young adolescents and the seasoned firefighters was so moving, but it was nothing compared to the day Cody walked into class holding a plastic bag. He walked over, handed it to me, and said, "My family and I have to get a lot of our meals from food banks, but we wanted to give something." In the bag was a can of whole-kernel yellow corn. While my desk was laden with home-cooked meals and delectable desserts, nothing held the beauty of that one can of Del Monte corn.

Another lesson that has stayed with me over the years came in the form of a baggie full of coins and bills. My seventh graders decided that they'd like to do something meaningful for the holiday season, and we settled on raising money for Heifer International, a global nonprofit that works to eliminate poverty and hunger through sustainable community development. We sold trinkets, involved the entire school by collecting money in individual classrooms, and asked for donations from the community. We were close to reaching our goal, but collections had tapered off when Felix pushed us over the top. One morning, he came in the door, walked over, and plunked a baggie full of cash down on my desk. He said it was all the money he'd earned from mowing lawns that summer, and he'd saved it to buy presents for his family. At dinner the night before, he'd asked his parents and brother if they'd be okay if he instead donated the money to our project. It struck me that Felix had chosen to give everything he possibly could. What a life lesson for all of us.

One of the more ambitious charitable endeavors involved a nonprofit preschool a few blocks over from our middle school. I'd volunteered to teach an elective that year, and I decided to focus on getting out into the community. The preschool did amazing work, serving an intentionally crafted student population of special needs and typical children. The school's mission was to provide a nurturing, educational environment for children of all physical and mental abilities. Each class was comprised of an equal number of special needs and typical children. My students decided to volunteer a few times each week in the various classrooms, reading books, singing, dancing, whatever a group of twelve- and thirteen-year-olds could do to contribute. It wasn't long before my students began to talk to me about how worn down the building and supplies were from years of use. Before I knew it, we were knee deep in donations that included toys, books, art supplies, labor, wall paint, and money. The director of the center just kept saying over and over that she couldn't believe how the kids just "got it"—how they saw a need, stepped in, and did something about it. By the time that school year ended, many relationships had been forged and lasting memories made.

Every year, the seniors in my high school program were able to apply for a one-of-a-kind scholarship. A family in the community had lost their son to suicide at the age of eighteen, and they chose to honor him by forming a nonprofit foundation that raised money for the graduating seniors in the program. We took every opportunity to help the foundation raise money as well, whether it was through collecting money from the community or asking for donations at various events. I think this was especially meaningful because the kids were able to serve a cause that impacted their own community. The freshmen, sophomores, and juniors looked forward to becoming seniors so that they could apply for a scholarship that had by that time become important to them.

When we were still unable to attend school face-to-face because of Covid, I was teaching remotely, and I'd assigned all of my high school students a project of their choosing. The grandmother of one of my students had died very recently, and she came to me with an idea to help other elderly people who were isolated, like her grandmother had been, due to the pandemic. She started a program called "Sunshine on a Covid Day" and had other students begin writing letters and cards to older individuals that we identified by reaching out to our community. Several elementary schools heard about it, and soon we were taking armfuls of colorful cards and pictures to assisted living facilities and other businesses that worked with an elderly population. The program eventually expanded beyond our community's boundaries and even beyond the borders of our country. Students became pen pals with older people from—literally—all over the world.

The kids eventually began writing to struggling teens as the long months of Covid dragged on and on. I was able to see firsthand how much this meant to the recipients of the letters. My cousin had just gotten out of the hospital after a stem cell transplant when her husband was diagnosed with terminal cancer. The letters they received from my students were treasured, shared with anyone who came to visit, and read over and over. I was amused when I realized how few of my kids knew how to address a letter. Some even asked me which side the stamp went on! It was a reminder that today's teenagers have limited experiences of personal correspondence, with texting as their go-to form of communication.

The last thing I want to say on the topic of giving is that I learned not to be afraid to ask for the things I needed for the classroom. I've always been touched by how people respond when it's kids who need something. I've seen the members of my community sponsor students and their families for the holidays, donate furniture, and give food to my classroom pantry. During the school year after we returned to face-to-face learning following Covid, I was working with a high school's gifted and talented center, and we were in desperate need of classroom supplies. I put a few messages out on social media, and the outpouring was astounding! If there was a special trip or event planned and I asked for help for students who couldn't afford it, the community always came through. *People want to help.* They don't always know how, but when they see a need, they respond. I am always grateful for the lesson my students learn when they see that complete strangers care about them.

I Am

I am an ordinary, uninteresting guy
I wonder what people think of me
I hear nothing, except for my thoughts, free as can be
I see people who are so successful that they practically fly
I want to be like them, soaring in the sky
I am an ordinary, uninteresting guy.

I pretend that I don't care about what others think
I feel my emotions pilling up, like dishes in a sink
I touch a rag, trying to wash them all away
I worry that the dishes will get too high, that I won't be able to
make them stay
I cry when I try to hide my emotions and lie
I am an ordinary, uninteresting guy.

I understand that I think too lowly of myself
I say that everything will be fine
I dream of making all I want mine
I try to follow those dreams
I hope that life isn't as it seems
I am an ordinary, uninteresting guy.

—Grant, age fourteen

Chapter 16

People First

One lesson that I've learned over the years, regardless of the age or grade, is the value of getting to know our students as people. There have been times when my own knowledge of a student's situation made the difference between a situation being resolved peacefully or spinning out of control. My favorite example of this is Ian.

I first met Ian when he came to shadow at our high school when he was an eighth grader. I've taught enough children who have a diagnosis of Autism Spectrum Disorder (ASD) that I can spot them immediately, and I absolutely *love* these kids. From the first moment I encountered the lanky teen with hair falling into his eyes, his ankle-length jeans exposing his white socks, I knew he was one of those wonderfully quirky individuals that I'd remember forever.

The first day of his freshman year, Ian and I had our first of many spirited encounters over his laptop. He seemed incapable of leaving it for more than a few minutes, and I took to sitting beside him during class when students were working independently in order to monitor his behavior. It didn't take long for me to realize that he was writing code and creating complicated computer programs, and in just a few months, he'd created a personal website to advertise my side career as a public speaker. At fourteen, Ian was more advanced with computers than any adult I'd ever encountered.

One of the more challenging aspects of teaching Ian was his lack of social skills. I can't tell you how many times I had to remind him that hovering right at my shoulder wasn't okay when I was conferencing with another student. At other times, I'd be diligently working at my computer and sense that my boy was near. If I didn't acknowledge him right away, it wouldn't take long for him to crane his neck around my shoulders and peer directly into my eyes. He never spoke, just stared. It always reminded me of the robot from *Flight of the Navigator.* But how I loved him!

During the second semester of Ian's freshman year, Colorado Public Radio's education reporter came to our classroom to do a story about the program I co-taught. Ian was determined to be interviewed, and—in typical Ian fashion—he followed the reporter around long enough that she finally asked if he wanted to talk. He wound up being featured prominently in her story, and his picture was front and center in the article published on the CPR website.

As luck would have it, the day after the CPR visit, Ian went to an advanced technology workshop for students who'd been nominated by their teachers due to their prowess with all things computer-related. The day after he returned, I was called to my principal's office, and when I walked in, someone from the district's Instructional Technology department was there, along with all of my building's administrators. A CPR executive was also present. It was quite a gathering.

When I sat down, they told me they wanted to talk to me about my student, Ian. It seemed that he'd decided to test out some of the new skills he'd acquired in the technology workshop and had hacked into CPR's website, as well as their vice president's personal email account. Everyone in the room was ready to come down hard on him, and words such as suspend, expel, and prosecute were being floated. I finally stopped them and said, "Okay. If Ian did this, he thought he was being helpful, I guarantee you. What did he do when he hacked in?" They all glanced at one another, and the CPR executive finally said that Ian had left (digital) notes behind, letting them know that if he, a high school freshman, was able to get in so easily, they needed to consider upgrading their security. He went on to tell us that Ian had even suggested various software programs that would be more secure than what they were currently using. Ian ended his advice with his name, email, and phone number, in case they wanted further assistance from him.

I didn't even have to say, "I told you so." Everyone realized that there was no malicious intent, and—while we needed to deal with the situation—nothing beyond a conference with Ian and his parents was needed. The IT director even remarked that with a little coaching, Ian was going to wind up making more money than anyone else in the room, adding that organizations like the FBI and the military were always looking for people with his skill set. This entire situation was a good reminder to me of the importance of knowing our students. The fact that I was aware of the technological lens through which Ian viewed the world turned the tide in a meeting that could have gone much differently. The world is going to benefit from the gifts in his brain, but it would have been so easy to overlook who Ian was and focus on the violation alone. We might have missed out on the opportunity to benefit from his abilities.

Teaching Tidbit Lesson 6:
Is There a Doctor in the House?

When a second grader is leaning back in her chair while holding a newly sharpened pencil, she may lose her balance and fall forward—impaling the pencil in her neck. It will turn out to be only a surface injury, but when the pencil is still stuck in the student's neck as you walk her to the office, it will bob up and down in rhythm to her (hysterical) sobs. *Note: there is a bonus here. The rest of the class will never, ever lean back in their chairs again without this event flashing through their mind. Your need to continually tell them to put all four chair legs on the floor 677 times a day will drop to only 223.*

Bathroom sinks can come off the wall and slice a student's hand open. Many stitches could be needed.

Never use a paper cutter when you're in a hurry to get straws cut for a Thanksgiving craft with your kindergarten class. Rushing makes it easy to chop off the end of your thumb. Again, stitches will be your friend.

If you work with younger students during a pandemic, be prepared for masks to be saturated by lunchtime. And I don't mean only with saliva.

It is possible for lice to infest eyelashes. If you ever find yourself in a situation where this is a possibility, use a magnifying glass. Unfortunately, you will never unsee it.

I Am

I am everything i need
I wonder if i am on the right path
I hear my love for this life, pounding in my head
i see my world ever expanding
I want to be authenic, the version of me that i have always
dreamed of
I am everything i need
I pretend to be someone i am not
I feel myself pulled towards an idea of myself, a person i have not
yet become
I touch pen to paper and draw myself in flight
I worry that my feet will never leave the ground
I cry when i feel bound to a person that i no longer am
I am everything i need
I understand that i can become self sufficient, that one day all i
will need is my own love to keep me warm
I say that i am a work in progress, learning to love myself once
more
I dream of a day where i am content with myself
I try to be gentle with my own heart
I hope for peace within my own mind
I am everything i need

-Ash, age eighteen

Chapter 17

Lessons of a Pandemic

"I wish it need not have happened in my time," said Frodo. "So do I,"
said Gandalf, "and so do all who live to see such times."
—J. R. R. Tolkien

Friday, March 13, 2020. News of the coronavirus was every-where, and school closings were looking inevitable. I decided to teach a lesson on various plagues that day, hoping to encourage students with examples of how the world has carried on after other devastating diseases. I included a lot of random trivia and fun facts. This was when grocery store shelves were quickly emptied of toilet paper, and stories of people fighting in the aisles over the last roll were becoming appallingly familiar. I ended the lesson that day with the story of the ancient Roman "communal sponge on a stick" that was kept in a bucket in their bathhouses. (If you're unfamiliar with this, look it up. You're welcome.) It was such a relief to have fun together, even in the face of such stress and uncertainty, and to reflect on history's lessons about resilience. Little did I know, it would be my last in-person lesson for over a year and a half.

Just before the end of school that day, we were told to take home everything we might need for a few weeks because our district was closing due to Covid. The closure was anticipated to last no longer than two weeks, three at the most. Rayne was a student in the last class of the day. A good example of "still waters run deep," Rayne's mind could absorb the most complex math problems ever invented. He always chose to sit in the back of the room, and I got such a kick out of teasing him to make him laugh or blush, preferably (and usually) both. Whenever he had a few free minutes in class, Rayne worked on fixing a complicated line of code he was writing. Who am I kidding . . . half of the time, he did it *instead* of his classwork, but I figured he was probably accomplishing something that would outlive us all, so I pretended not to notice.

Rayne never tried to draw attention to himself, which is why I was so surprised to find him still in the room after school ended that Friday afternoon. When I asked him what he needed, he simply said, "I just wanted to say 'bye.'" I gave him what turned out to be the last hug I'd be able to give any of my students for several years because this was the day life changed for us all . . . our last day of in-person learning. I wish I'd known how long it would be before we would be together again. Rayne seemed to have a sixth sense about what was ahead, and I'm grateful he listened to his intuition so that my last memory was of him scurrying out of the room with a red but happy face because Mama Lee had once more embarrassed him with a big hug. In the weeks and months that followed, I often wished I'd had the chance to spend a minute or two with each of my kids before 3:00 p.m. on that Friday the 13th.

I'd have told my freshmen how much their sparkle, energy, and lack of sophistication made our short time together so memorable. I'd have told my sophomores how much I appreciated and admired their leadership, creativity, and the way they supported one another. I'd have told my juniors how glad I was that it wasn't my last year with them and that I was going to make sure we squeezed every ounce of goodness possible out of their senior year. Oh, and yes, my 2020 seniors. Honestly, I'd have spent most of the time just looking at their faces. Remembering how different they looked when they walked into the classroom as deer-in-the-headlights freshmen. I'd watch the movies of their antics that I've stored up in my mind . . . listening to them share while standing on "Speak Your Truth Rock" at the fall retreats, attending the school board meeting that lasted until 4:00 a.m. during their freshman year in order to fight for funding, haranguing them about blowing off assignments and opting instead to socialize, confiscating phones (after snapping a selfie of me with the student to send to their parents when they were on them during class,) and watching them display their creativity in full at various school events. Most of all, I replayed the "movies" of how they made their lasting mark on our school community. Impressive class presentations and not-so-impressive ones, baseball in the snow, lunchtimes with ongoing Dungeons and Dragons, some tears . . . and lots and lots of laughter.

And the weeks turned into months as remote learning became the norm. One of my students was a varsity cheerleader, and while we were in quarantine, she did a fall project about how Covid affected her sport. She called it "Covid's Effect on Cheer." When I read the title, I couldn't help but think of the double meaning, since my own cheer was quickly evaporating. I felt like a one-dimensional version of myself; no matter how dynamic the lesson was, regardless of the hours of rich online discussions, it was just so hard. How do you build relationships using a keypad and a mouse? There was always that blasted glass screen between me and the faces I loved. My administration thought I was a successful remote learning teacher, and I believe I did the very best job possible, but I never stopped yearning for a return to the classroom with my kids.

One day I was so "school sick" that I drove to my school, let myself in, and climbed the steps down to the lower level where my empty classroom waited. I just sat there and wrote the following:

There's not much lonelier than a schoolhouse devoid of students. I sat down on the stool at the front of the room. Waiting. The first echo I heard was laughter. Loud, raucous guffaws. Timid giggles. Moments of pure joy. I heard your voices. Speaking your truth, expressing your dreams, sharing your heartaches. I felt your energy, the passion of your convictions, your hunger for social justice. I saw you there. Loaded down with a backpack full of too-heavy books, carrying a Monster drink in one hand and your phone in the other. I ached for the chance to tell you to put down your blasted device and get ready for class. You are my people. You give me such hope. And although the events of today will be a memory before we know it, today I feel your absence so keenly. Yet, as I left the building behind, I no longer noticed the emptiness of the place. Instead, I was overcome with gratitude that this is my world, and it will be waiting when the time is right. I miss you, my tribe.

As Winnie the Pooh said, "How lucky I am to have had something that makes saying goodbye so hard." Eventually, we all adjusted and adapted and came out on the other side. Today, I honestly hope we never get back to the "normal" of life before the pandemic. The lessons we learned as students, teachers, and humans living in a global pandemic changed us. I hope that after this experience, we never take being together with other people for granted. And when we were finally back together, I was so incredibly glad to be able to hug again!

Teaching Tidbit Lesson 7:
Things That Make Me Go Hmmm

After Covid, there was a lot of concern about the learning loss
our children experienced. At the same time, teachers were
leaving the profession in record numbers due to overwhelming
workloads, lack of public support, extreme stress, and low pay.
Talk about a learning loss!

When there is such emphasis on differentiating for our students,
why are we then required to give them standardized tests?

When elementary school students get in trouble for being too
physically active in class, why are they made to miss recess as a
punishment?

Isn't it a bit counterintuitive to send students home for a few days
as a punishment for skipping classes?

When I made a lateral move that meant I would no longer be
in the classroom, everyone referred to it as a "promotion," even
though there was no change in pay or title. I always thought a
promotion was when one was elevated to a higher role within an
organization. Why in the world would leaving the classroom be
considered a "promotion"?

Education colleges used to be called "normal schools," and that
is just such a great thing.

I Am

I am hopeful and creative.
I wonder what our purpose is
I hear the laughter of the cheerful
I see a world of possibilities
I want to make a difference
I am hopeful and creative.

I pretend life is perfect
I feel the need of change
I touch the stars
I worry that people lose sight of their goals
I cry when cruelty goes unpunished
I am hopeful and creative.

I understand our time is limited
I say the world needs change
I dream of a world where everyone has a chance
I try to make a difference
I hope for the world to be better when I leave it
I am hopeful and creative.

—Allaire, age ten

Chapter 18

It's a Jungle in Here!

Sometimes, it's more than the people who make our lives worthwhile. Maybe it's because I was raised "in the country" where not having animals around was more abnormal than having ten or twenty in your house. I was riding a horse before I got my first bicycle and was chased by my Aunt Ferrell's rooster more than once. For years, I rationalized my classroom zoo by telling myself how good it was for my students to have the responsibility of taking care of living creatures, but the truth was that I couldn't imagine a classroom without them. Some of the animals were wilder than others, but lessons came from each one. I'd like to think that no matter how many years have passed, my kids remember the fun we had playing with and taking care of our classroom menageries.

It wasn't spring unless we had new life emerging in all corners of the room, whether it was tadpoles metamorphosing into frogs a bit at a time or painted lady butterflies emerging from their chrysalis prisons. By far, though, the most anticipated spring animals were the ducklings we'd hatch in our incubator. When the first little pecks broke through the eggs, we were transfixed, watching nature's creation miracle unfold. One year, we had a particularly successful hatch of a dozen ducklings that comprised three different varieties. Once they were old enough to swim, we'd take them every morning to the pond we'd built. Teachers would bring their classes out to watch the ducklings splash and play. It was something the whole school community looked forward to each spring.

Our Title I school was participating in a pilot program, and one day, a group of executives from the company who wrote the curriculum, as well as upper-level district administrators, had gathered in the library to discuss how the program was progressing. It was truly a group of Folks We Want to Impress. It was time for our daily pilgrimage to the pond, and we set off, passing by the library on the way. The class of first graders knew to follow my student teacher down the hall while I stationed myself at the very end, behind the ducklings that waddled behind the class in single file. Our principal pointed out the orderly progression of adorable six-year-olds to the group of Important People, and everyone paused to watch them walk by. Imagine their surprise when, behind the line of humans, a peeping group of multicolored ducklings brought up the rear!

Crabby and Gabby were a bonded pair of cockatiels that produced quite a few offspring that we'd hand-feed from the time they hatched. Quite often, we'd let Crabby and Gabby out of their cage, and students hardly noticed them perching on various pieces of furniture as we went about our day. One afternoon, the principal came in for a formal observation. My students were all seated crisscross applesauce on the alphabet rug in our reading corner as I read aloud. As was often the case, Crabby and Gabby were hanging out on the back of a nearby chair as I read, and it was one of those moments when I felt like The Most Inspirational Educator On Earth. Yet, even with my mesmerizing lesson, I could tell my principal was distracted; his eyes kept darting over to look at the birds. I finally realized that they'd decided it was time to expand their little family, and they were working hard at it. I stopped, not quite sure what to say, but before I opened my mouth, one of my second graders said, "Oh look, Crabby and Gabby are going to have more babies!" That was all; they then turned back to me, ready to hear the end of the story, and I continued with my lesson. My principal gave me the best rating I'd ever gotten on an observation.

A favorite pet was Rainbow, a sun conure whose daily dances were a highlight for all of us. We'd put on music, begin to chant "Go Rainbow, Go Rainbow!" and he'd bob his head up and down while he moved his legs from side to side in rhythm to the music. Rainbow traveled back and forth from school with me each day, perched on my shoulder as he gazed out the car window. As someone who gets cold very easily, if the temperature is below fifty, I crank the heat. Some days, I'd realize that the car was stifling when he'd lean around so he was looking me right in the eye, open his beak wide, and dramatically pant as a hint that it was WAY too hot, even for a tropical bird!

If I had meetings after school, he went with me, even if they weren't in my building. I always say I hope I die in that type of meeting because the difference between life and death would be so subtle that I wouldn't even know I'd crossed over, but at least Rainbow brought some levity. Once, when I was in a meeting at our district offices with a group of people who took themselves very seriously, Rainbow was snoozing, tucked up under my shirt, and no one sitting around the large conference table even knew he was there. Until, that is, he began headbutting against my top to get out. I pretended not to notice, and I could tell everyone was trying very hard not to stare at my pulsating chest. Finally, he worked his way to the top of my shirt and POP! Out came his head, swiveling from side to side as he took in his surroundings. It was a glorious moment, and I didn't even get reprimanded!

When he was only a few years old, Rainbow developed a brain tumor, and I eventually had to have him euthanized. My third graders were crushed, and we planned an elaborate funeral and burial next to our school pond. Each student brought something to the service to leave in the hole we'd dug for Rainbow's "coffin," and when they dropped it in, they said their own personal goodbyes to our beloved, colorful little bird. I've been to many funerals in my life, but I've never seen one more authentic than the one we gave Rainbow that afternoon. And to this day, I can't hear Gwen Stefani's "Hollaback Girl" without seeing Rainbow getting his groove on.

One year's extreme pets earned our class the nickname "Lee's Zoo Crew." We had an aquarium full of fish, a cage of finches, Crabby and Gabby, a parakeet, a guinea pig named Flo Jo, and Bailey Bunny. But the most memorable and favorite of them all was Wendy Flower, our skunk. And before I go on, yes, you CAN de-scent one, although I typically acted surprised that it was possible when someone asked me if I'd "taken the stink out." Wendy Flower had the run of the room, was litter box trained, and liked nothing more than to curl up in a lap and sleep. I have a memorable story that involves a faculty happy hour, Wendy Flower, a huge outside deck just right for a skunk to slip under, a panicked skunk owner commando-crawling for yards and yards under said deck, and hot firefighters, but that's another story for another book.

I've had more than my share of classroom bunnies, but the most memorable was a pair of female rabbits. I got them at the beginning of the year from the family of one of my students, and they were wilder than others I'd owned. I felt like it wasn't right to keep two almost feral rabbits caged, so after a couple of months, we let them go in the shady, enclosed courtyard down the hall from our classroom. The kids and I would go down several times a day to keep them company, leaving food and water and check-ing on their newly dug burrows, and, by all accounts, they were settling in nicely. Over Christmas break, the custodial crew kept them fed and watered, and when we came back in January, I was eager to see how they were doing, but before I could make it up the hallway, a teacher came in and asked me if "all of those rabbits" were mine. Since everyone knew who the bunnies belonged to, I was surprised at the question, but when I just said yeah, we had a brown and black one living in the courtyard, she asked who all the other ones belonged to.

Along with my entire class, I hurried down the hall to check things out, and there in the courtyard, we learned firsthand that the rabbits were *not* both females. Instead, they were a proud mom and dad of eight adorable balls of fluff. My students became expert rabbit catchers that month. We advertised in the neighborhood that we had free rabbits, and when we got a request, we'd all head to the courtyard. The kids took up positions around the courtyard, with two of them covering the tops of the burrows to keep any babies from escaping underground. The rest of us scattered to the corners and along the edges of the courtyard, and together we'd form a human dragnet, spreading out to make the capture. It became the highlight of every day, and the last two rabbits we caught were the parents. Once the virile papa bunny got his baby-making parts removed, the two lived happily in the courtyard for a long time afterward. But we all missed the fun of the chase, not to mention the cuteness overload that eight little bunnies brought.

Another memorable time when we failed to keep a classroom pet contained involved a little teddy bear hamster named Theodore Roosevelt. My elementary-school students loved him, and he liked nothing more than to be cuddled up in someone's shirt. One Friday, his cage didn't get closed all the way, and when we returned to school on Monday, Theo was nowhere to be found. I was afraid to alert my administration about the situation, confident we'd find him before anyone was the wiser. And find him we did—first, in the room directly across the hall.

By the time we had calmed everyone down and the screaming had subsided, Theo had once again disappeared into the wall. He'd travel from room to room, in no particular sequence, but the panic had subsided from his first sighting now that everyone knew the scratching in the walls that they kept hearing wasn't a rat colony descending on the school. Several times a day, I'd hear, "It's Theodore Roosevelt!" and we'd know he'd once again made an appearance. This went on for several weeks until Theo was finally captured in the art room, at which time the principal imposed a new rule that no one could have any classroom pets smaller than an elephant. Well, perhaps that is a bit of an exaggeration, but what I can say with authority is that Theodore Roosevelt was relegated to my home, and there he lived out his life without ever escaping again.

Not all the animals that have lived within my classroom walls were domesticated, nor were they all pets. A teacher once brought in a teeny baby rabbit that she'd rescued from her cat, and my students and I bottle-fed it until it was big enough to be released. We once took in a chipmunk with a wounded leg, nursing him back to health until he was ready to return to the pine trees outside of our classroom. Injured baby birds, a turtle with a gash on its neck, and even a baby squirrel that had fallen out of the nest all somehow found their way to my classrooms over the years, and I'd like to think that the experience of caring for helpless, often injured creatures helped my students grow in compassion as they learned to nurture them back to health.

It seems remiss not to at least acknowledge some of the other animals that have made their mark on my career. Daisy May the ferret, who loved to curl up and sleep inside our shoes . . . Pongo and Luna bunnies . . . Franklin Delano Roosevelt, a leopard gecko whose lack of intelligence was surpassed only by his tolerance as he was passed from hand to hand . . . Mr. Peanut Butter and Klef, the sweetest pet rats you could ever meet . . . the baby tarantulas that we watched change and grow . . .

And then there is the praying mantis story. Like any good first-grade teacher, I had an interactive science table off to the side of my classroom. I was always on the lookout for cool "sciency" things to add to the collection. One day, I was delighted to find an empty praying mantis cocoon in my garden. Not only did I have these beneficial insects living among my tomatoes and corn, but I also had a new treasure to display on my science table. A few weeks later, as I was teaching a writing lesson, I saw one of my most active, rambunctious first-grade boys standing by the science table, turning round and round, hands clapped to the top of his head. In my best teacher voice, I demanded that he sit down and join in the activity we were all working on. He just looked at me and, throwing his arms wide, said in a bemused voice, "They're EVERYWHERE!" Sure enough, the "empty" cocoon had erupted, and several hundred baby praying mantises had begun crawling all over the classroom. (And yes, I mean several hundred. I Googled it. Those suckers have a lot of babies at one time.) We carefully gathered up as many of the insects as we could and transported them to our butterfly garden, but we found a few every day for weeks afterward, hidden in books in the reading nook and among the math manipulatives, and each time we'd make the pilgrimage to the garden to give them a new start in life.

Mahatma Gandhi said, "The greatness of a nation and its moral progress can be judged by the way its animals are treated." In some communities where I've taught, pets were more likely to be neglected than abused. One day, a friend drove a pair of brothers home after school. As she walked them to the door, they pointed to the area behind their apartments and said, "That's our dog." She looked over, and lying on the ground was a decaying carcass of what had once been a family pet. I'd like to think that, even in such communities, my students' experiences taking care of creatures who were totally dependent on them for survival made a difference for animals they'd encounter in the future.

Teaching Tidbit Lesson 7:
You Won't Learn This in College

You can Google how to take out the ink reservoir from a high-lighter and replace it with contraband. Those were some smart seventh graders.

Sometimes, "educrats" become so obsessed with instructional minutes that they outlaw recess and limit field trips. And when they do approve an excursion, they'll require you to teach a lesson on the bus while traveling to and from the venue.

It's possible for an ice storm to come in so quickly that you have to spend the night at school with elementary students. It's especially fun when the power goes out.

While teaching kindergarten and first grade, you may begin to call yourself "Mr. Door" or "Ms. Door," because students will tap on you. All. Day. Long.

If you're teaching primary students, replacing shoestrings with Velcro may seem to be a small thing, but it will give you back hours of your day.

Secretaries run the school. This can't be emphasized enough.

Middle school students fall out of their chairs often. They run into things often. They trip over their own feet. Often.

When you teach in a less-than-safe area, a pool may be formed in which the faculty bets on which staff member's car will be stolen next.

Elementary, middle, and high school teachers take on the characteristics of their students.

You will never keep up with the current teen slang. Stop trying.

It could be that you'll spend time in courtrooms testifying on behalf of your students, whether it is for Child Protective Services, prosecution for a violent attack, or guardianship. And you may find that judges love educators.

A HUGE perk of teaching high school is students who bring in your favorite coffee when they're late for first period, knowing your gratitude will keep you from marking them tardy for the fifteenth time that week.

You should always volunteer for bus dismissal duty on the last day of school. There is no feeling like it in the world.

Chapter 19

School of Hard Knocks

As you read my words, it might be easy to assume that I never had any difficult days while teaching, but the truth is that I not only had difficult *days,* I also had *weeks* and sometimes *months* in which I struggled. Whether it was because of my own shortcomings, administrative conflicts, parents who didn't approve of my teaching style, or students with whom I didn't see eye-to-eye, I know what it's like to get up and not want to go to work. Thankfully, over a career spanning decades, the difficult times were far outweighed by the wonderful ones.

Most of the time, when I hit a rough patch, I played a definite part in the problem. I was able to own my actions and change the things that had led to the situation. And although forgiving myself was always the hardest part, I could learn and move on. The last time I found myself in a difficult situation wasn't terribly long ago, and I did a lot of soul-searching about my own part in it. Much of the time I teach with my sense of humor at the forefront, and as an extrovert I know that there are times when my exuberance is a bit over the top. In this particular instance, one of my teenage students had been offended by something I'd said during a lesson. He didn't come to me right away, and it grew from a few hurt feelings into one that had him "recruiting" others in his resentment. Teenagers tend to have a strong sense of justice, and when he approached some extremely vulnerable students, things escalated. Parents and district officials got involved, and although almost all the students eventually apologized, except for the instigator, and expressed feelings about how inappropriate the attack was, it took a while for the situation to settle down. I eventually determined that while I might be responsible for a small piece, and took ownership of it, the situation was mostly just downright mean. How could this happen to someone who had given her entire being to this profession? Finally, I decided that I was supposed to walk through the fire so that I could understand when others went through similar hard times. If I want to be a person who inspires and encourages others who are teaching or considering teaching as a career, I need to experience it all, the good and the bad.

It's easy to be excited about a piece of artwork when the creativity and passion are flowing. The brushstrokes are clean, the colors vibrant, and personal satisfaction overflows. But when the colors run together into a muddy blur, when the product begins to morph far from your vision, it's hard to find your way back to your original inspiration. But if I'm sincerely committed to being a "real teacher," I have to accept that I'm not perfect, and neither are any of the people around me. Difficult times are inevitable when you're working closely with your fellow human beings. This particular situation brought me to my knees, and I struggled for quite a while. But I finally made myself look beyond those who had caused me pain. I thought about the ones who loved me unconditionally, in spite of my shortcomings. I remembered the times I had watched my students grow and change right in front of me. And I centered myself on the knowledge that I will always be a work in progress, that the canvas will never truly be a finished work. I accepted that I'll always respond deeply when painful situations arise because I am so intensely anchored in the work. If I want to experience exhilarating highs and meaningful connections, I have to be willing to hurt sometimes, even if the situation is not of my own making.

When I became a teacher, I had no idea that such difficulties were ahead. The regret about the mistakes I've made remains with me, even though I work hard at giving myself the same grace I hope others afford me. The residual pain of being treated unfairly pops up from time to time. But I also didn't know about the way my work would complete me. I had no idea how this profession would ultimately shape me in every area of my life. In spite of the painful experiences that shook my confidence, I'd still make the same choice to become a real teacher every time.

One of the gut-wrenching realities of teaching is that we are not able to reach every student we teach. When we go into this profession, we do so with the belief that we can and will make a difference. But there are those for whom the magic doesn't happen. For some, the world they experience outside of school is too powerful. When I was teaching fourth grade in an inner-city Atlanta neighborhood, I had a reputation for reaching the most difficult students, but I definitely fell short with some. On the first day of fourth grade, Rico walked through the door with a swagger and a sneer. During a class bathroom break, he was slouching around the hall, refusing to get in line so we could go to lunch. In my best this-is-the-beginning-of-the-year-and-I-must-make-a-positive-but-firm-impression voice, I told him—yet again—to get in line. He turned and said, "F*#% you!" That set the tone for his entire fourth-grade year. He was already involved in a gang and went by the street name "Lil' Man." When I had conferences with his mother to discuss my concerns about Rico's behavior, she was defensive, convinced that I didn't understand her son. She laughed at the idea of his involvement in a gang. Ten years later, Rico shot and killed two police officers, and the media detailed his gang membership and nickname on the street . . . Lil' Man.

Sometimes the battles students wage internally must take precedence. I've worked with students whose depression and anxiety were so debilitating that their attempts to stay in school failed, in spite of an intense desire to succeed . . . to be "normal." After a challenging middle school experience, Erin came to me her freshman year, eager for a fresh start. She would come to class, draw her knees up to her chest, and practically vibrate with anxiety. She wanted to succeed, and I wanted it for her—so much. After just one semester, I received an email from her parents thanking me for working with their daughter. They had decided to withdraw and homeschool her because her anxiety had become so debilitating. During the semester that Erin was with me, I so desperately wanted to reach her. To help her see herself through my eyes. To calm that horrible monster that dictated her days. The knowledge that I couldn't left me feeling empty. I was able to follow Erin as she progressed through school, and she eventually enrolled in a community college to finish out her high school career. Seeing her succeed made me so proud, but I still resent the power of the anxiety that plagued her.

Sometimes, the damage is too great, and our students are so protected by layers of armor that it's virtually impossible to reach them. When I began teaching Lucas in eighth grade, he had a reputation for challenging authority and openly defying anyone who tried to help him. His stepfather was a violent man whose main child-rearing strategies were deprivation and humiliation. Lucas would come to school with stories of punishments like being forced to weed with a spoon for hours on end and having everything in his bedroom taken away except a mattress. He'd be forced to sit ramrod straight on that mattress for hours on end. Lucas was incredibly bright, talented, funny, creative . . . he had so many qualities that should have been treasured and nurtured. Our relationship was intense, in both positive and negative ways, but I loved him fiercely. Ultimately, though, that love wasn't enough to give him the self-esteem and confidence to break through that tough shell he'd built around himself. Today I wear a charm on my lanyard that he made me in art class, a heart with a peace sign in the middle. He broke my heart.

There are no college or professional development classes that can prepare you for a suicidal student. Most educators go into teaching because we care and want to make a better future for those who pass in and out of our classrooms every day. When a student decides that there is no future for them, there is just no way to process it. Knowing that they have reached such a deep level of despair makes it hard to breathe. When we are confronted with the reality that there is pain so deep it can't be reached even by the most dedicated, talented teachers in our ranks or the most loving families, it is exquisitely and profoundly sad.

Over the last decade, I have visited more students in locked psychiatric wards than anyone would believe. Anxiety, depression, drug addiction, alcoholism, bulimia, self-harm . . . the list goes on and on. Society is deeply failing our most troubled young people, but that is a book in and of itself. Some of my students came very close to ending their pain, but only one, an eighth grader, "successfully completed" the act. The last time I saw her, I remember thinking how empty she looked behind her eyes. There were many events in the time leading up to her death that indicated the depth of her pain, but in spite of everyone's best efforts, she felt that this was her best option for finding peace. That wound remains open for many of us who knew her.

One night, I got a call about a sophomore who had run away from home days before. He was texting his closest friends to say good-bye, and he only made it to a crisis center because an astute police officer noticed that he'd been riding the same light rail train all day. Sweet, sensitive, kind, witty, and wicked smart, he had also been diagnosed with severe depression, anxiety, and dissociative disorder. His eighth-grade year was spent in a school for students for whom emotional support is more important than academics. On his good days, I called him Tigger because he could be in his seat one minute and across the room the next, entertaining his friends. On the days that he struggled, he sat in his seat pulled into a ball, physically and emotionally far away from the rest of us. He came back after several weeks away, but it wasn't long before he was in serious legal trouble and placed in a youth correctional facility. I still miss him.

No educator has found a magic cure for every troubled student that crosses their path. From one educator to another, I give you permission to not reach them all, and if I can say that to you, then I have to give myself the same grace and understanding. Give your best, do all you are capable of doing, and let it be enough. Honestly, those I failed to reach still haunt me. Admitting that I failed a child goes against everything I stand for. But I have learned that if I focus on those experiences too much, I'm not able to be there for the rest. When we allow those who are not in a place to be helped to dominate our energy, we end up being no good to anyone. Sometimes we have to accept that it will take more than our efforts to save a child. And that's okay. Mostly.

Developed in 2009 and rolled out in 2010, the Common Core is a group of mathematics and English language arts/literacy standards created to ensure that all high school graduates are equipped with the knowledge and skills necessary for future success. States adopted these high-quality standards, and regardless of where students lived, the Common Core aimed to provide a consistent curriculum instead of the varied state-by-state standards that were the norm in education. Opinions differ as to the success of the Common Core, and today more and more states are implementing new educational standards to take its place. But regardless of its success or lack thereof, I'm not writing about the Common Core in an academic sense.

From the first moment I heard the term, my first thought was that I'd already been teaching the "common core" since August 1987. You see, I believe that in spite of our differences, we are capable of finding something in each person that unites us in our humanity. This has guided my teaching more than any other belief. When I first began my career, I thought I'd develop a bond with every student I taught, but as with all relationships, we are more drawn to some people than others. There have been students along the way that I felt I never connected with, and I know there are those who didn't relate to my teaching style. As hard as it is to admit, some of my students just flat out didn't like me. But even the rough-around-the-edges kids deserved my best, and I always tried to give it. Sometimes, I really had to dig to find a common core, but if I really looked, it was there. That doesn't mean I didn't have difficult moments with challenging students. I just tried to connect at a heart level whenever possible.

Educators will not be the only ones who read my book. I hope this message can resonate with people from all walks of life. I feel honored that you've chosen to read about my journey. The common core standards of the human heart connect us. And for that, I am grateful.

I Am

I am of hardships and new beginnings.
I wonder what people think of their lives and of others
I hear the laughter of the young and the yearning of the old
I see the scars inflicted by a harmful intention, and
I want to replace those intentions with an innate self-love
I am of hardships and new beginnings.

I pretend that I do not hold judgment and disdain for hypocriti-
cal feelings
I feel as though selflessness isn't a virtue, even if it can be
I touch the face of someone I don't know but love—craving
through the glass that is not there
I worry that I hurt those I wish to savor and keep sound
I cry when lives end and when lives begin to go astray (but do
they really go astray?)
I am of hardships and new beginnings.

I understand that others feel pain from things I do not, but still
spite them
I say that life is not life without a purpose and an acceptance of
simply living
I dream that someday we will all see the ripples of the ocean, not
the ripples of the blood shed in a heart
I try to give others what they are searching for and
I hope that they are not desires, but rose buds that will bloom
into something to outlive them
I am of hardships and new beginnings.
—Kat, age thirteen

Chapter 20

A Universal Language

Not long after my first TEDx Talk about "real teachers" was uploaded, I received an email asking if I'd be interested in taking that message to Turkey, serving as the keynote speaker at the country's largest educational conference, held annually in Izmir. While I was beyond honored and excited about the opportunity, it was a bit daunting to prepare a presentation for an audience whose first language was not English. For some of them, it was not even their *second* language. Although I spent countless hours revising my keynote address, fretting over the nuances of the English language, and wondering which stories would lose their relevance, it turned out I needn't have worried. There was a definite language difference, but it sure wasn't a barrier.

Using my favorite John Steinbeck quotes about real teachers, I spoke for an hour and a half to over a thousand Turkish educators. They laughed with me, we wiped away tears together, and we batted beach balls around the room while Farrell Williams's song "Happy" blared through the speakers. But most of all, we celebrated that we were fortunate enough to have been called to this profession.

I'll never forget the faces as I looked out at the audience while I was speaking. The smiles, the connections—it had a palpable power. Their love for teaching came off them in waves. After the session, a line wound around the auditorium as teachers waited to have a picture taken with me. Almost to a person, they'd tell me that they, like me, were a "real teacher." For almost two hours, I posed for pictures, hugged, and gave thanks that the children of Turkey were in such good hands. It was an experience that I could never have prepared for, and the lesson I learned that day will be with me forever: the power and love of teaching don't need a common language to be shared.

And so it is.

I Am

I am funny and weird
I wonder if monsters are real
I hear the voices of kids at night
I see the reflection of a man
I want world domination
I am funny and weird.

I pretend I'm an army man, hunting monsters late at night
I feel alive and energetic
I touch the scales of a black monster
I worry about natural disasters
I cry about losing someone I love
I am funny and weird.

I understand that 10 x 10 equals 100
I say aliens are real
I dream about living in a log cabin
I try to do my best on tests
I hope I become a Navy Seal
I am funny and weird.

—Andre, age ten

Chapter 21

The Next Chapter

So. Here we are at the end. You've heard the stories and met the students behind them You've read about the heartaches and celebrated the victories. I've thought about writing this book for years, and eventually, it took on a life of its own. It's a story that had to be told, for me, if for no one else. I hope that, above all else, the impact of the teaching profession has come through—how we are all changed in our work together, student and teacher. Steinbeck's words about his three "real teachers" have remained true for me for almost four decades. I hope I have left my students with the desire to know more, as well as the courage to face their fears. And the truth that I hope I left them with is the knowledge that we are all capable of changing the world around us, even a teacher from a small town in the deep South.

Have you ever made a decision that you *knew* was the right one, yet it also broke your heart? In March 2021, I made the decision to begin a new adventure, one that wouldn't take place within the four walls of a classroom. After almost thirty-four years . . . I took the opportunity to become a resource teacher for my school district. Although I had never lost my love of teaching, I knew it was time to try something different. Whether in the form of moving from elementary to middle school or changing my subject from English to social studies, I've always needed change in my career.

The longest I've ever stayed in one school is seven years—I've always listened when the restlessness indicating my readiness for a different challenge begins to rumble deep inside. But I had never made a change as drastic as this one. Had Covid never happened, I'm not sure I'd ever have been able to make such a change, but since I'd taught remotely for a year and a half, there was a degree of separation that I needed in order to leave my people. Although I'd felt pretty successful in the relationships that I had sustained and built during Covid, the experience could never take the place of the daily routines of face-to-face teaching.

When I announced my new position, I was struck by something that I would hear several times. Although this was a lateral move in terms of pay and position—I was moving from classroom teacher to a "teacher on special assignment"—I'd often be congratulated on my "promotion." It was weird that others considered it a promotion when I moved from daily interactions with kids to a position where that wasn't an expectation. I certainly didn't look at it like that, and while I didn't see it as a demotion, either, I still wondered why people saw getting away from the kids as a move up in my career.

The fall semester of 2021 saw me living in a fog of nostalgia and heartache, and I eventually realized that if I was going to make a difference in this new position, I had to break up with teaching. It truly was like deciding to leave a relationship with someone that I was still in love with. It was time, the decision was right, and yet, it was one of the most painful things I've ever experienced. I no longer knew how to answer when asked what it was that I did. Was I still a teacher? It was the one identity I'd never doubted or regretted. So who was I now without a group of kids to call my own? I took time to mourn the loss, worked hard on changing my attitude, and forged on. But I'll never be able to think of myself as anything except what I was born to be: a real teacher. There is no calling that is more sacred.

I Am

I am a real teacher.
I wonder if my words touched your heart
I hear the passage of time beating in my ears
I see a fire lighting inside of you
I want you to give it your all
I am a real teacher.
I pretend my best is enough.
I feel the words on every page.
I touch your hidden potential
I worry that you'll give up
I cry when someone is lost to us
I am a real teacher.
I understand that I was called to teach
I say I wouldn't change a thing
I dream about changing my corner of the world
I try to inspire others to do the same
I hope you are never satisfied with mediocrity
I am a real teacher.

—Lisa Lee

Acknowledgements

There are so many people behind this book, both directly and indirectly. It's overwhelming to consider the support, encouragement, and love that surrounds me. I'm humbled and filled with gratitude.

Since this wouldn't even exist without them, so much love goes out to the decades of kids who have taught me so much.

I owe a debt of gratitude to all of those who have worked with me in the trenches. So many of you have become lifelong friends, and you've influenced my craft in so many positive ways.

For all of my educators who shaped me as a learner, but most importantly as a human, I'll always be paying it forward.

There are some beautiful women who gave me the chance to be a mom. I love you all!

My Fab Four, Soon-to-be-Five. Thank you for keeping your grandma young.

For those who held the lamp aloft in front of me during the dark years, your light will forever shine for and in me.

Kathleen, thank you for pushing past my resistance to help me become a more whole person.

I'm so grateful to my sister along with my K.A.L.L. pack, for reading my words and giving honest feedback.

Lastly, I'll never be able to find the right words to thank my publisher, Journey Institute Press. Michael and Dafna, you are my Change Agents. Since our first meeting nine years ago, my dreams have materialized.

About the Author

Lisa Lee is a 35-year veteran educator with the honors of being named "Teacher of the Year" in DeKalb County, Georgia (2007) and Runner-Up "Teacher of the Year" for Colorado (2017). Over the years, Lisa Lee has taught in Georgia and Colorado elementary, middle, and high school classrooms, with a specialization in Gifted and Talented and a focus on the students who don't always fit in a box. An experienced TEDx speaker, Lisa embraces the TEDx platform as a gateway to deliver her messages of connection and relationship building that she so strongly believes in.

Her personal life philosophy is that "We're put here on the planet to make life better for others. Period." This belief is the foundation of her messaging in that making connections with others and building community can change lives. Lisa lives in the Denver, CO area with her wife, 2 grandtwins, and her dog Rosa Barks.

Journey Institute Press

Journey Institute Press is a non-profit publishing house created by authors to flip the publishing model for new authors. Created with intention and purpose to provide the highest quality publishing resources available to authors whose stories might otherwise not be told.

JI Press focusses on women, bipoc, and lgbtq+ authors without regard to the genre of their work.

As a Publishing House, our goal is to create a supportive, nurturing, and encouraging environment that puts the author above the publisher in the publishing model.

Mind Flash Publishing is an Imprint of Journey Institute Press, a Division of 50 in 52 Journey, Inc.

Mind Flash Publishing

Printed in the USA
CPSIA information can be obtained
at www.ICGtesting.com
LVHW022113011123
762552LV00082B/221/J